THE  OF KNOWING CHRIST

MEDITATIONS ON THE GOSPELS

POPE BENEDICT XVI

THE *Joy* OF KNOWING CHRIST

MEDITATIONS ON THE GOSPELS

POPE BENEDICT XVI

the WORD among us® press

Published by The Word Among Us Press
9639 Doctor Perry Road
Ijamsville, Maryland 21754
www.wordamongus.org
14 13 12 11 10   4 5 6 7 8
ISBN: 978-1-59325-151-2

Scripture texts used in this work, as well as Pope Benedict XVI's homilies and
addresses, are taken from the Vatican translation and
can be found on the Vatican Web site, www.vatican.va.
Used with permission of Libreria Editrice Vaticana.

Cover design by John Hamilton Design
Cover photo of Pope Benedict XVI Catholic News Service.
Used with permission.

Library of Congress Cataloging-in-Publication Data

Benedict XVI, Pope, 1927-
The joy of knowing Christ : meditations on the Gospels / Pope Benedict XVI.
    p. cm.
ISBN 978-1-59325-151-2 (alk. paper)
1. Bible. N.T. Gospels--Meditations. 2. Jesus Christ--Meditations. I. Title.
BS2555.54.B46 2009
242'.5--dc22
                                                    2008040314

CONTENTS

EDITOR'S PREFACE

The words, "Rejoice, because God is with you; he is with us," are words that truly open a new epoch. Dear friends, with an act of faith we must once again accept and understand in the depths of our hearts this liberating word: "Rejoice!"

—Pope Benedict XVI

As Pope Benedict XVI notes in the first meditation in this collection, knowing that there is a God who is good, who knows us, who is so near to us, is truly the gospel—the good news that brings us joy.

And the Holy Father is the bearer of good news in these fifty-five reflections on passages from the gospels. Taken from his homilies and Angelus messages over the past three years, the meditations here reveal the pope's passionate love for Christ, his depth of faith, his grasp of Scripture, and his perspective on the challenges facing us as Christians in the world today. Pope Benedict is a brilliant theologian and scholar, but first and foremost he is a pastor, and this is evident in every meditation in this collection. A strong advocate of *lectio divina*, the prayerful reading of the Scriptures, he shows us how much nourishment and inspiration we can derive from meditating on the word of God.

The Word Among Us Press is delighted to bring you these reflections. We hope that as you meditate on the gospels with Pope Benedict, you will experience the great joy of which he speaks—that of knowing Christ and his overflowing love for you, his beloved son or daughter.

1. Introduction:
Reading Scripture in the Spirit

On November 18. 1965, the Second Vatican Ecumenical Council approved the Dogmatic Constitution on Divine Revelation, *Dei Verbum*. This document is one of the pillars on which the entire council is built. It addresses Revelation and its transmission, the inspiration and interpretation of sacred Scripture and its fundamental importance in the life of the Church.

Gathering the fruits of the theological renewal that preceded it, Vatican II put Christ at the center, presenting him as "both the mediator and the sum total of Revelation" (*Dei Verbum*, 2). Indeed, the Lord Jesus, the Word made flesh who died and rose, brought to completion the work of salvation, consisting of deeds and words, and fully manifested the face and will of God so that no new public revelation is to be expected until his glorious return (see DV, 3).

The apostles and their successors, the bishops, are depositories of the message that Christ entrusted to his Church so that it might be passed on in its integrity to all generations. Sacred Scripture of the Old and New Testaments and sacred Tradition contain this message, whose understanding develops in the Church with the help of the Holy Spirit.

This same Tradition makes known the integral canon of the sacred books. It makes them directly understandable and operative so that God, who has spoken to the patriarchs and prophets, does not cease to speak to the Church and, through her, to the world (see DV, 8).

The Church does not live for herself but for the gospel, and it is always in the gospel that she finds the direction for her journey.

The conciliar constitution *Dei Verbum* emphasized appreciation for the Word of God, which developed into a profound renewal for the life of the eccclesial community, especially in preaching, catechesis, theology, spirituality, and ecumenical relations. Indeed, it is the Word of God which guides believers, through the action of the Holy Spirit, toward all truth (see John 16:13).

Among the many fruits of this biblical springtime I would like to mention the spread of the ancient practice of *lectio divina* or "spiritual reading" of sacred Scripture. It consists in poring over a biblical text for some time, reading it and rereading it, as it were, "ruminating" on it as the Fathers say and squeezing from it, so to speak, all its "juice," so that it may nourish meditation and contemplation and, like water, succeed in irrigating life itself.

One condition for *lectio divina* is that the mind and heart be illumined by the Holy Spirit, that is, by the same Spirit who inspired the Scriptures, and that they be approached with an attitude of "reverential hearing."

This attitude was typical of Mary Most Holy, as the icon of the annunciation symbolically portrays: the Virgin receives the heavenly messenger while she is intent on meditating upon the sacred Scriptures, usually shown by a book that Mary holds in her hand, on her lap or on a lectern.

This is also the image of the Church which the council itself offered in the constitution *Dei Verbum*: "Hearing the Word of God with reverence . . ." (1).

Let us pray that like Mary, the Church will be a humble handmaid of the divine Word and will always proclaim it with firm trust, so that "the whole world . . . through hearing it may believe, through belief . . . may hope, through hope . . . may come to love" (DV, 1).

—Angelus, November 6, 2005

2. Sharing Mary's Joy
Luke 1:26-28

R ejoice!"

Let us now meditate briefly on . . . one of the loveli-est passages of sacred Scripture. And so as not to take too long, I would like to reflect on only three words from this rich gospel.

The first word on which I would like to meditate with you is the angel's greeting to Mary. In the Italian translation the angel says, "Hail, Mary." But the Greek word *kaire* means in itself "be glad" or "rejoice."

And here is the first surprising thing: the greeting among the Jews was "Shalom," "Peace," whereas the greeting of the Greek world was *Kaire*, "Be glad." It is surprising that the angel, on entering Mary's house, should have greeted her with the greet-ing of the Greeks: *Kaire*, "Be glad, rejoice." And when, forty years later, the Greeks had read this gospel, they were able to see an important message in it: they realized that the beginning of the New Testament, to which this passage from Luke referred, was bringing openness to the world of peoples and to the uni-versality of the People of God, which by then included not only the Jewish people but also the world in its totality, all peoples.

The new universality of the kingdom of the true son of David appears in this Greek greeting of the angel.

However, it is appropriate to point out straightaway that the angel's words took up a prophetic promise that is found in the book of the prophet Zephaniah. We find the same greeting almost literally. Inspired by God, the prophet Zephaniah says to Israel, "Shout for joy, O daughter Zion! . . . the LORD [is with you and] is in your midst." We know that Mary was very familiar with the sacred Scriptures. Her Magnificat is a fabric woven of threads from the Old Testament. We may thus be certain that the Blessed Virgin understood straightaway that these were the words of the prophet Zephaniah addressed to Israel, to the "daughter Zion," considered as a dwelling place of God. And now the surprising thing, which must have given Mary food for thought, is that these words, addressed to all Israel, were being specifically addressed to her, Mary. And thus, it must clearly have appeared to her that she herself was the "daughter Zion" of whom the prophet spoke, and that the Lord, therefore, had a special intention for her, that she was called to be the true dwelling place of God, a dwelling place not built of stones but of living flesh, of a living heart, that God was really intending to take her, the Virgin, as his own true temple. What an intention! And as a result, we can understand that Mary began to think with special intensity about what this greeting meant.

However, let us now reflect in particular on the first word: "Rejoice, be glad." This is the first word that resounds in the New Testament as such, because the angel's announcement to Zechariah of the birth of John the Baptist is the word that still rings out on the threshold between the two Testaments. It is only with this dialogue which the angel Gabriel has with Mary that the New Testament really begins. We can therefore say that the first word of the New Testament is an invitation to joy: "Rejoice, be glad!" The New Testament is truly "gospel," the "good news" that brings us joy. God is not remote from us, unknown, enigmatic or perhaps dangerous. God is close to us, so close that he makes himself a child, and we can informally address this God.

It was the Greek world above all that grasped this innovation, that felt this joy deeply, for it had been unclear to the Greeks whether there was a good God, a wicked God, or simply no God. Religion at that time spoke to them of so many divinities: therefore, they had felt they were surrounded by very different divinities that were opposed to one another; thus, they were afraid that if they did something for one of these divinities, another might be offended and seek revenge.

So it was that they lived in a world of fear, surrounded by dangerous demons, never knowing how to save themselves from these forces in conflict with one another. It was a world of fear, a dark world. Then they heard: "Rejoice, these demons are nothing; the true God exists and this true God is good, he loves us, he knows us, he is with us, with us even to the point that he took on flesh!"

This is the great joy that Christianity proclaims. Knowing this God is truly "good news," a word of redemption.

Perhaps we Catholics who have always known it are no longer surprised and no longer feel this liberating joy keenly. However, if we look at today's world where God is absent, we cannot but note that it is also dominated by fears and uncertainties: Is it good to be a person or not? Is it good to be alive or not? Is it truly a good to exist? Or might everything be negative? And they really live in a dark world; they need anesthetics to be able to live. Thus, the words, "Rejoice, because God is with you, he is with us," are words that truly open a new epoch.

Dear friends, with an act of faith we must once again accept and understand in the depths of our hearts this liberating word: "Rejoice!" We cannot keep solely for ourselves this joy that we have received; joy must always be shared. Joy must be communicated. Mary went without delay to communicate her joy to her cousin Elizabeth. And ever since her assumption into heaven, she has showered joy upon the whole world; she has become the great Consoler: our Mother who communicates joy, trust, and kindness and also invites us to spread joy. This is the real commitment of Advent: to bring joy to others. Joy is the true gift of Christmas, not expensive presents that demand time and money.

We can transmit this joy simply: with a smile, with a kind gesture, with some small help, with forgiveness. Let us give this joy, and the joy given will be returned to us. Let us seek in particular to communicate the deepest joy, that of knowing God in Christ. Let us pray that this presence of God's liberating joy will shine out in our lives.

—Homily, December 18, 2005

3. Falling into God's Hands
Luke 1:29-33

The second word on which I would like to meditate is another word of the angel's: "Do not fear, Mary," he says. In fact, there was reason for her to fear, for it was a great burden to bear the weight of the world upon herself, to be the mother of the universal King, to be the mother of the Son of God: what a burden that was! It was too heavy a burden for human strength to bear! But the angel said: "Do not fear! Yes, you are carrying God, but God is carrying you. Do not fear!"

These words, "Do not fear," must have deeply penetrated Mary's heart. We can imagine how in various situations the Virgin must have pondered those words; she must have heard them again.

At the moment when Simeon said to her, "This child is destined to be the downfall and the rise of many in Israel, a sign that will be opposed—and you yourself will be pierced with a sword," at that very moment in which she might have succumbed to fear, Mary returned to the angel's words and felt their echo within her: "Do not fear, God is carrying you." Then, when contradictions were unleashed against Jesus during his public life and many said, "He is crazy," she thought once again of the angel's words in her heart, "Do not fear," and went ahead.

Lastly, in the encounter on the way to Calvary and then under the cross, when all seemed to be destroyed, she again heard the angel's words in her heart: "Do not fear." Hence, she stood courageously beside her dying Son and, sustained by faith, moved toward the resurrection, toward Pentecost, toward the foundation of the new family of the Church.

"Do not fear": Mary also addresses these words to us. I have already pointed out that this world of ours is a world of fear: the fear of misery and poverty, the fear of illness and suffering, the fear of solitude, the fear of death. We have in this world a widely developed insurance system; it is good that it exists. But we know that at the moment of deep suffering, at the moment of the ultimate loneliness of death, no insurance policy will be able to protect us. The only valid insurance in those moments is the one that comes to us from the Lord, who also assures us: "Do not fear, I am always with you." We can fall, but in the end we fall into God's hands, and God's hands are good hands.

—Homily, December 18, 2005

4. Daring to Say Yes with Mary
Luke 1:34-38

The third word: at the end of the colloquium, Mary answered the angel, "I am the servant of the Lord. Let it be done to me as you say." Thus, Mary anticipated the Our Father's third invocation: "Your will be done." She said "yes" to God's great will, a will apparently too great for a human being; Mary said "yes" to this divine will, she placed herself within this will, placed her whole life with a great "yes" within God's will, and thus opened the world's door to God.

Adam and Eve, with their "no" to God's will, had closed this door. "Let God's will be done": Mary invites us too to say this "yes," which sometimes seems so difficult. We are tempted to prefer our own will, but she tells us: "Be brave, you too say: 'Your will be done,' because this will is good." It might at first seem an unbearable burden, a yoke impossible to bear; but in reality, God's will is not a burden; God's will gives us wings to fly high, and thus we too can dare, with Mary, to open the door of our lives to God, the doors of this world, by saying "yes" to his will, aware that this will is the true good and leads us to true happiness. Let us pray to Mary, Comfort of the Afflicted, our mother, the Mother of the Church, to give us the courage to say this "yes" and also to give us this joy of being with God and to lead us to his Son, to true life. Amen!

—Homily, December 18, 2005

5. God's Dwelling Place
Luke 1:39-45

On the eve of his passion, taking leave of his disciples, the Lord said, "In my Father's house are many rooms. . . . I go to prepare a place for you."

By saying, "I am the handmaid of the Lord; let it be done to me according to your word," Mary prepared God's dwelling here on earth; with her body and soul, she became his dwelling place and thereby opened the earth to heaven.

In the gospel we have just heard, St. Luke, with various allusions, makes us understand that Mary is the true Ark of the Covenant, that the mystery of the Temple—God's dwelling place here on earth—is fulfilled in Mary. God, who became present here on earth, truly dwells in Mary. Mary becomes his tent. What all the cultures desire—that God dwell among us—is brought about here.

St. Augustine says, "Before conceiving the Lord in her body, she had already conceived him in her soul." She had made room for the Lord in her soul, and thus really became the true temple where God made himself incarnate, where he became present on this earth.

Thus, being God's dwelling place on earth, in her the eternal dwelling place has already been prepared; it has already been prepared forever. And this constitutes the whole content of the dogma of the assumption of Mary, body and soul, into heavenly glory, expressed here in these words. Mary is "blessed" because—totally, in body and soul and forever—she became the Lord's dwelling place. If this is true, Mary does not merely invite our admiration and veneration, but she guides us, shows us the way of life, shows us how we can become blessed, how to find the path of happiness.

Let us listen once again to Elizabeth's words fulfilled in Mary's Magnificat: "Blessed is she who believed." The first and fundamental act in order to become a dwelling place of God and thus find definitive happiness is to believe: it is faith, faith in God, in that God who showed himself in Jesus Christ and makes himself heard in the divine Word of holy Scripture.

Believing is not adding one opinion to others. And the conviction, the belief, *that* God exists is not information like any other. Regarding most information, it makes no difference to us whether it is true or false; it does not change our lives. But if God does not exist, life is empty, the future is empty. And if God exists, everything changes, life is light, our future is light, and we have guidance for how to live. Therefore, believing constitutes the fundamental orientation of our life. To believe, to say: "Yes, I believe that you are God; I believe that you are present among us in the incarnate Son," gives my life a direction, impels me to be attached to God, to unite with God, and so to find my dwelling place, and the way to live.

—Homily, August 15, 2006

6. Mary, Mirror of God's Mercy
Luke 1:46-55

In the Magnificat, the great hymn of Our Lady that we have just heard in the gospel, we find some surprising words. Mary says: "Henceforth all generations will call me blessed." The Mother of the Lord prophesies the Marian praises of the Church for all of the future, the Marian devotion of the people of God until the end of time. In praising Mary, the Church did not invent something "adjacent" to Scripture; she responded to this prophecy which Mary made at that moment of grace.

And Mary's words were not only personal, perhaps arbitrary words. Elizabeth, filled with the Holy Spirit as St. Luke said, exclaimed with a loud cry: "Blessed is she who believed. . . ." And Mary, also filled with the Holy Spirit, continues and completes what Elizabeth said, affirming: "All generations will call me blessed." It is a real prophesy, inspired by the Holy Spirit, and in venerating Mary, the Church responds to a command of the Holy Spirit; she does what she has to do.

We do not praise God sufficiently by keeping silent about his saints, especially Mary "the Holy One" who became his dwelling place on earth. The simple and multiform light of God appears to us exactly in its variety and richness only in the countenance of the saints, who are the true mirrors of his light. And it is precisely by looking at Mary's face that we can see more clearly than in any other way the beauty, goodness, and mercy of God. In her face we can truly perceive the divine light.

"All generations will call me blessed." We can praise Mary, we can venerate Mary, for she is "blessed," she is blessed forever. And this is the subject of this feast [the Assumption of Mary]. She is blessed because she is united to God; she lives with God and in God.

—Homily, August 15, 2006

7. Fear of God

Luke 1:50

To believe is not only a way of thinking or an idea; . . . it is a way of acting, a manner of living. To believe means to follow the trail indicated to us by the Word of God. In addition to this fundamental act of faith, which is an existential act, a position taken for the whole of life, Mary adds another word: "His mercy is on those who fear him."

Together with the whole of Scripture, she is speaking of "fear of God." Perhaps this is a phrase with which we are not very familiar or do not like very much. But "fear of God" is not anguish; it is something quite different. As children, we are not anxious about the Father, but we have fear of God, the concern not to destroy the love on which our life is based.

Fear of God is that sense of responsibility that we are bound to possess, responsibility for the portion of the world that has been entrusted to us in our lives. It is responsibility for the good administration of this portion of the world and of history, and one thus helps the just building of the world, contributing to the victory of goodness and peace.

—Homily, August 15, 2006

8. God Made Himself Small for Us

Luke 2:8-20

"To you is born this day in the city of David a Savior, who is Christ the Lord. And this will be a sign for you: you will find a babe wrapped in swaddling clothes and lying in a manger" (Luke 2:11-12). Nothing miraculous, nothing extraordinary, nothing magnificent is given to the shepherds as a sign. All they will see is a child wrapped in swaddling clothes, one who, like all children, needs a mother's care; a child born in a stable, who therefore lies not in a cradle but in a manger. God's sign is the baby in need of help and in poverty. Only in their hearts will the shepherds be able to see that this baby fulfills the promise of the prophet Isaiah. . . : "For to us a child is born, to us a son is given; and the government will be upon his shoulder" (Isaiah 9:6). Exactly the same sign has been given to us. We too are invited by the angel of God, through the message of the gospel, to set out in our hearts to see the child lying in the manger.

God's sign is simplicity. God's sign is the baby. God's sign is that he makes himself small for us. This is how he reigns. He does not come with power and outward splendor. He comes as a baby—defenseless and in need of our help. He does not want to overwhelm us with his strength. He takes away our fear of his greatness. He asks for our love: so he makes himself a child. He wants nothing other from us than our love, through which we spontaneously learn to enter into his feelings, his thoughts, and his will—we learn to live with him and to practice with him that humility of renunciation that belongs to the very essence of love. God made himself small so that we could understand him, welcome him, and love him.

—Homily, December 24, 2006

9. Signs of God's Love

Luke 2:8-20

The Fathers of the Church, in their Greek translation of the Old Testament, found a passage from the prophet Isaiah that Paul also quotes in order to show how God's new ways had already been foretold in the Old Testament. There we read: "God made his Word short, he abbreviated it" (Isaiah 10:23; Romans 9:28). . . .

The Word which God speaks to us in Sacred Scripture had become long in the course of the centuries. It became long and complex, not just for the simple and unlettered, but even more so for those versed in sacred Scripture, for the experts who evidently became entangled in details and in particular problems, almost to the extent of losing an overall perspective. Jesus "abbreviated" the Word—he showed us once more its deeper simplicity and unity. Everything taught by the law and the prophets is summed up, he says, in the command: "You shall love the Lord your God with all your heart, and with all your soul, and with all your mind. . . . You shall love your neighbor as yourself" (Matthew 22:37-40). This is everything—the whole faith is contained in this one act of love which embraces God and humanity. Yet now further questions arise: how are we to love God with all our mind, when our intellect can barely reach him?

How are we to love him with all our heart and soul, when our heart can only catch a glimpse of him from afar, when there are so many contradictions in the world that would hide his face from us? This is where the two ways in which God has "abbreviated" his Word come together. He is no longer distant. He is no longer unknown. He is no longer beyond the reach of our heart. He has become a child for us, and in so doing, he has dispelled all doubt. He has become our neighbor, restoring in this way the image of man, whom we often find so hard to love. For us, God has become a gift. He has given himself. He has entered time for us. He who is the eternal One, above time, has assumed our time and raised it to himself on high. Christmas has become the feast of gifts in imitation of God who has given himself to us.

Let us allow our heart, our soul, and our mind to be touched by this fact! Among the many gifts that we buy and receive, let us not forget the true gift: to give each other something of ourselves, to give each other something of our time, to open our time to God. In this way anxiety disappears, joy is born, and the feast is created. During the festive meals of these days, let us remember the Lord's words: "When you give a dinner or a banquet, do not invite those who will invite you in return, but invite those whom no one invites and who are not able to invite you" (see Luke 14:12-14). This also means: when you give gifts for Christmas, do not give only to those who will give to you in return, but give to those who receive from no one and who cannot give you anything back. This is what God has done: he invites us to his wedding feast, something which we cannot reciprocate, but can only receive with joy. Let us imitate him! Let us love God and, starting from him, let us also love man so that, starting from man, we can then rediscover God in a new way!

And so, finally, we find yet a third meaning in the saying that the Word became "brief" and "small." The shepherds were told that they would find the child in a manger for animals, who were the rightful occupants of the stable. Reading Isaiah (1:3), the Fathers concluded that beside the manger of Bethlehem there stood an ox and an ass. At the same time they interpreted the text as symbolizing the Jews and the pagans—and thus all humanity—who each in their own way have need of a Savior: the God who became a child. Man, in order to live, needs bread, the fruit of the earth and of his labor. But he does not live by bread alone. He needs nourishment for his soul; he needs meaning that can fill his life. Thus, for the Fathers, the manger of the animals became the symbol of the altar, on which lies the Bread which is Christ himself: the true food for our hearts. Once again we see how he became small: in the humble appearance of the host, in a small piece of bread, he gives us himself.

All this is conveyed by the sign that was given to the shepherds and is given also to us: the child born for us, the child in whom God became small for us. Let us ask the Lord to grant us the grace of looking upon the crib this night with the simplicity of the shepherds so as to receive the joy with which they returned home (see Luke 2:20). Let us ask him to give us the humility and the faith with which St. Joseph looked upon the child that Mary had conceived by the Holy Spirit. Let us ask the Lord to let us look upon him with that same love with which Mary saw him. And let us pray that in this way, the light that the shepherds saw will shine upon us too, and that what the angels sang that night will be accomplished throughout the world: "Glory to God in the highest, and on earth peace among men with whom he is pleased." Amen!

—Homily, December 24, 2006

10. LIGHTING THE WAY FOR OTHERS
MATTHEW 2:1-12

Today ... we joyfully celebrate the Epiphany of the Lord, his manifestation to the peoples of the entire world, represented by the Magi who came from the East to render homage to the King of the Jews. Observing the heavenly phenomena, these mysterious personages had seen a new star and, instructed by the ancient prophets as well, they recognized in it the sign of the Messiah's birth, a descendant of David (see Matthew 2:1-12). From its initial appearance, therefore, the light of Christ began to attract to himself the people "with whom he is pleased" (Luke 2:14), of every tongue, people, and culture. It is the power of the Holy Spirit that moves hearts and minds to seek truth, beauty, justice, peace. It is what the Servant of God John Paul II affirmed in the encyclical *Fides et Ratio*: "Men and women are on a journey of discovery which is humanly unstoppable—a search for the truth and a search for a person to whom they might entrust themselves" (33). The Magi found both of these realities in the Child of Bethlehem.

Men and women of every generation need on their pilgrim journey to be directed: what star can we therefore follow? After coming to rest "over the place where the child was" (Matthew 2:9), the purpose of the star that guided the Magi ended, but its spiritual light is always present in the Word of the gospel, which is still able today to guide every person to Jesus. This same Word, which is none other than the reflection of Christ, true man and true God, is authoritatively echoed by the Church for every well-disposed heart. The Church too, therefore, carries out the mission of the star for humanity. But something of the sort could be said of each Christian, called to illuminate the path of the brethren by word and example of life. How important it is that we Christians are faithful to our vocation! Every authentic believer is always traveling his own personal itinerary of faith and, at the same time, with the little light that he carries within himself, can and must be a help to those alongside him, and even a help to the one for whom finding the way that leads to Christ is difficult.

—Angelus, January 6, 2008

11. THE EVIDENCE OF REPENTANCE
MATTHEW 3:1-12

Today . . . presents to us the austere figure of the precursor, whom the Evangelist Matthew introduces as follows: "In those days came John the Baptist, preaching in the wilderness of Judea: 'Repent, for the kingdom of heaven is at hand'" (Matthew 3:1-2). His mission was to prepare and clear the way for the Lord, calling the people of Israel to repent of their sins and to correct every injustice. John the Baptist, with demanding words, announced the imminent judgment: "Every tree, therefore, that does not bear good fruit is cut down and thrown into the fire" (3:10). Above all, John put people on guard against the hypocrisy of those who felt safe merely because they belonged to the chosen people; in God's eyes, he said, no one has reason to boast but must bear "fruit that befits repentance."

. . . John the Baptist's appeal for conversion rings out in our communities. It is a pressing invitation to open our hearts to receive the Son of God, who comes among us to make manifest the divine judgment. The Father, writes John the Evangelist, judges no one but has given all judgment to the Son because he is the Son of Man (see John 5:22, 27). And it is today, in the present, that our future destiny is being played out. It is our actual conduct in this life that decides our eternal fate. At the end of our days on earth, at the moment of death, we will be evaluated on the basis of our likeness—or lack of it—to the Child who is about to be born in the poor grotto of Bethlehem, because he is the criterion of the measure that God has given to humanity. The heavenly Father, who expressed his merciful love to us through the birth of his only begotten Son, calls us to follow in his footsteps, making our existence, as he did, a gift of love. And the fruit of love is that fruit which "befits repentance," to which John the Baptist refers while he addresses cutting words to the Pharisees and Sadducees among the crowds who had come for baptism.

Through the gospel, John the Baptist continues to speak down the centuries to every generation. His clear, harsh words are particularly salutary for us, men and women of our time, in which the way of living and perceiving Christmas unfortunately all too often suffers the effects of a materialistic mind-set. The "voice" of the great prophet asks us to prepare the way of the Lord, who comes in the external and internal wildernesses of today, thirsting for the living water that is Christ. May the Virgin Mary guide us to true conversion of heart, so that we may make the necessary choices to harmonize our mentalities with the gospel.

—Angelus, December 9, 2007

12. Witnessing to Truth and Love
John 1:19-34

John the Baptist was the forerunner, the "voice" sent to proclaim the incarnate Word. Thus, commemorating his birth actually means celebrating Christ, the fulfillment of the promises of all the prophets, among whom the greatest was the Baptist, called to "prepare the way" for the Messiah (see Matthew 11:9-10).

All the gospels introduce the narrative of Jesus' public life with the account of his baptism by John in the River Jordan. . . . My book *Jesus of Nazareth* also begins with the baptism of Jesus in the Jordan, an event which had enormous echoes in his day. People flocked from Jerusalem and every part of Judea to listen to John the Baptist and have themselves baptized in the river by him, confessing their sins (see Mark 1:5).

The baptizing prophet became so famous that many asked themselves whether he was the Messiah. The Evangelist, however, specifically denied this: "I am not the Christ" (John 1:20). Nevertheless, he was the first "witness" of Jesus, having received instructions from heaven: "He on whom you see the Spirit descend and remain, this is he who baptizes with the Holy Spirit" (1:33).

This happened precisely when Jesus, after receiving baptism, emerged from the water: John saw the Spirit descending upon him in the form of a dove. It was then that he "knew" the full reality of Jesus of Nazareth and began to make him "known to Israel" (John 1:31), pointing him out as the Son of God and Redeemer of man: "Behold, the Lamb of God, who takes away the sin of the world!" (1:29).

As an authentic prophet, John bore witness to the truth without compromise. He denounced transgressions of God's commandments, even when it was the powerful who were responsible for them. Thus, when he accused Herod and Herodias of adultery, he paid with his life, sealing with martyrdom his service to Christ who is Truth in person.

Let us invoke his intercession, together with that of Mary Most Holy, so that also in our day the Church will remain ever faithful to Christ and courageously witness to his truth and his love for all.

—Angelus, June 24, 2007

13. IMMERSED IN LOVE
MATTHEW 3:13-17

The Child, who the Magi from the East came to adore at Bethlehem offering their symbolic gifts, we now find an adult, at the time when he is baptized in the Jordan River by the great prophet John (see Matthew 3:13). The gospel notes that after Jesus had received baptism and left the water, the heavens opened and the Holy Spirit descended on him like a dove (see 3:16). Then a voice was heard from heaven that said: "This is my beloved Son, with whom I am well pleased" (3:17). This was his first public manifestation after approximately thirty years of hidden life at Nazareth. Besides the Baptist, eyewitnesses of the singular event were the Baptist's disciples, some of whom then became Christ's followers (see John 1:35-40). It is both a christophany and a theophany: first of all, Jesus manifests himself as the *Christ*, a Greek translation of the Hebrew *Messiah*, which means "anointed." He was not anointed with oil as were Israel's kings and high priests, but rather with the Holy Spirit. At the same time, together with the Son of God appeared signs of the Holy Spirit and the heavenly Father.

What is the meaning of this act that Jesus wishes to fulfill— overcoming the Baptist's resistance—in order to obey the Father's will (see Matthew 3:14-15)? The profound sense emerges only at the end of Christ's earthly existence, in his death and resurrection. Being baptized by John together with sinners, Jesus began to take upon himself the weight of all of humanity's sin, like the Lamb of God who "takes away" the sin of the world (see John 1:29): an act which he brought to fulfillment on the cross when he also received his "baptism" (see Luke 12:50). In fact, by dying he is "immersed" in the Father's love and the Holy Spirit comes forth, so that those who believe in him could be reborn by that inexhaustible font of new and eternal life. Christ's entire mission is summed up in this: to baptize us in the Holy Spirit, to free us from the slavery of death, and "to open heaven to us," that is, access to the true and full life that will be "a plunging ever anew into the vastness of being, in which we are simply overwhelmed with joy" (*Spe Salvi,* 12).

. . . [Let us] pray for all Christians, so that they may understand the gift of baptism ever more and apply themselves to live it coherently, witnessing to the love of the Father and of the Son and of the Holy Spirit.

—Angelus, January 13, 2008

14. Overcoming Satan's Temptations
Mark 1:12-15

Today the gospel reminds us that Jesus, after being baptized in the River Jordan and impelled by the Holy Spirit who settled upon him and revealed him as the Christ, withdrew for forty days into the desert of Judea where he overcame the temptations of Satan (see Mark 1:12-13). Following their Teacher and Lord, Christians also enter the Lenten desert in spirit in order to face with him the "fight against the spirit of evil."

The image of the desert is a very eloquent metaphor of the human condition. The Book of Exodus recounts the experience of the people of Israel who, after leaving Egypt, wandered through the desert of Sinai for forty years before they reached the promised land.

During that long journey, the Jews experienced the full force and persistence of the tempter, who urged them to lose trust in the Lord and to turn back; but at the same time, thanks to Moses' mediation, they learned to listen to God's voice calling them to become his holy people.

In meditating on this biblical passage, we understand that to live life to the full in freedom, we must overcome the test that this freedom entails, that is, temptation. Only if he is freed from the slavery of falsehood and sin can the human person, through the obedience of faith that opens him to the truth, find the full meaning of his life and attain peace, love, and joy.

—Angelus, March 5, 2006

15. A PASSION FOR GOD'S REIGN
MATTHEW 4:12-23

Matthew . . . presents the beginning of Christ's public mission. It consisted essentially in preaching the kingdom of God and healing the sick, showing that this kingdom is close at hand and is already in our midst. Jesus began his preaching in Galilee, the region where he grew up, the "outskirts" in comparison with the heart of the Jewish nation, which was Judea, and in it, Jerusalem. But the prophet Isaiah had foretold that this land, assigned to the tribes of Zebulun and Napthali, would have a glorious future: the people immersed in darkness would see a great light (see Isaiah 8:22–9:2). In Jesus' time, the term "gospel" was used by Roman emperors for their proclamations. Independent of their content, they were described as "good news," or announcements of salvation, because the emperor was considered lord of the world and his every edict as a portent of good. Thus, the application of this phrase to Jesus' preaching had a strongly critical meaning, as if to say God, and not the emperor, is Lord of the world, and the true gospel is that of Jesus Christ.

The "good news" which Jesus proclaims is summed up in this sentence: "The kingdom of God—or kingdom of heaven—is at hand" (see Matthew 4:17; Mark 1:15). What do these words mean? They do not of course refer to an earthly region marked out in space and time, but rather to an announcement that it is God who reigns, that God is Lord and that his lordship is present and actual, it is being realized. The newness of Christ's message, therefore, is that God made himself close *in him* and now reigns in our midst, as the miracles and healings that he works demonstrate. God reigns in the world through his Son made man and with the power of the Holy Spirit who is called "the finger of God" (Luke 11:20). Wherever Jesus goes, the Creator Spirit brings life, and men and women are healed of diseases of body and spirit. God's lordship is thus manifest in the human being's integral healing. By this, Jesus wanted to reveal the face of the true God, the God who is close, full of mercy for every human being; the God who makes us a gift of life in abundance, his own life. The kingdom of God is therefore life that asserts itself over death, the light of truth that dispels the darkness of ignorance and lies.

Let us pray to Mary Most Holy that she will always obtain for the Church the same passion for God's kingdom which enlivened the mission of Jesus Christ: a passion for God, for his lordship of love and life; a passion for man, encountered in truth with the desire to give him the most precious treasure: the love of God, his Creator and Father.

—Angelus, January 27, 2008

16. SEEK AND FIND
JOHN 1:35-42

The beauty of [Ordinary Time] . . . lies in the fact that it invites us to live our ordinary life as a journey of holiness, that is, of faith and friendship with Jesus continually discovered and rediscovered as Teacher and Lord, the Way, the Truth, and the Life of man.

This is what John's gospel suggests to us in today's liturgy when it presents the first meeting between Jesus and some of those who were to become his apostles. They had been disciples of John the Baptist, and John himself directed them to Jesus when, after baptizing him in the Jordan, he pointed him out as "the Lamb of God" (John 1:36).

Two of his disciples then followed the Messiah, who asked them, "What are you looking for?" The two asked him, "Teacher, where do you stay?" And Jesus answered, "Come and see," that is, he invited them to follow him and stay with him for a while. They were so impressed in the few hours that they spent with Jesus that one of them, Andrew, said to his brother Simon, "We have found the Messiah." Here are two especially important words: "seek" and "find."

From the page of today's gospel, we can take these two words and find a fundamental instruction in them for the new year: we would like it to be a time when we renew our spiritual journey with Jesus, in the joy of ceaselessly looking for and finding him. Indeed, the purest joy lies in the relationship with him, encountered, followed, known, and loved, thanks to a constant effort of mind and heart. To be a disciple of Christ: for a Christian, this suffices. Friendship with the Teacher guarantees profound peace and serenity to the soul, even in the dark moments and in the most arduous trials. When faith meets with dark nights, in which the presence of God is no longer "felt" or "seen," friendship with Jesus guarantees that, in reality, nothing can ever separate us from his love (see Romans 8:39).

To seek and find Christ, the inexhaustible source of truth and life: the Word of God asks us to take up, at the beginning of the new year, this never-ending journey of faith. We too ask Jesus, "Teacher, where do you stay?" and he answers us, "Come and see." For the believer, it is always a ceaseless search and a new discovery, because Christ is the same yesterday, today, and forever, but we, the world and history, are never the same, and he comes to meet us to give us his communion and the fullness of life. Let us ask the Virgin Mary to help us to follow Jesus, savoring each day the joy of penetrating deeper and deeper into his mystery.

—Angelus, January 15, 2006

17. HEALED FOR SERVICE
MARK 1:29-39

The Lord went to the house of Simon Peter and Andrew and found Peter's mother-in-law sick with a fever. He took her by the hand and raised her, the fever left her, and she served them.

Jesus' entire mission is symbolically portrayed in this episode. Jesus, coming from the Father, visited people's homes on our earth and found a humanity that was sick, sick with fever, the fever of ideologies, idolatry, forgetfulness of God. The Lord gives us his hand, lifts us up, and heals us.

And he does so in all ages; he takes us by the hand with his Word, thereby dispelling the fog of ideologies and forms of idolatry. He takes us by the hand in the sacraments; he heals us from the fever of our passions and sins through absolution in the Sacrament of Reconciliation. He gives us the possibility to raise ourselves, to stand before God and before men and women. And precisely with this content of the Sunday liturgy, the Lord comes to meet us; he takes us by the hand, raises us, and heals us ever anew with the gift of his words, the gift of himself.

But the second part of this episode is also important. This woman who has just been healed, the gospel says, begins to serve them. She sets to work immediately to be available to others, and thus becomes a representative of so many good women, mothers, grandmothers, women in various professions, who are available, who get up and serve and are the soul of the family, the soul of the parish. . . .

Moreover, women were the first messengers of the word of God in the gospel; they were true evangelists. And it seems to me that this gospel, with this apparently very modest episode, is offering us . . . an opportunity to say a heartfelt "thank you" to all the women who care for the parish, the women who serve in all its dimensions, who help us to know the Word of God ever anew, not only with our minds, but also with our hearts.

—Homily, February 5, 2006

18. Mary, the Model Intercessor
John 2:1-3

Mary makes a request of her son on behalf of some friends in need. At first sight, this could appear to be an entirely human conversation between a mother and her son, and it is indeed a dialogue rich in humanity. Yet Mary does not speak to Jesus as if he were a mere man on whose ability and helpfulness she can count. She entrusts a human need to his power—to a power which is more than skill and human ability. In this dialogue with Jesus, we actually see her as a Mother who asks, one who intercedes.

. . . It is worth going a little deeper, not only to understand Jesus and Mary better, but also to learn from Mary the right way to pray. Mary does not really ask something of Jesus; she simply says to him: "They have no wine" (John 2:3). Weddings in the Holy Land were celebrated for a whole week; the entire town took part, and consequently, much wine was consumed. Now the bride and groom find themselves in trouble, and Mary simply says this to Jesus. She doesn't ask for anything specific, much less that Jesus exercise his power, perform a miracle, produce wine. She simply hands the matter over to Jesus and leaves it to him to decide what to do. In the simple words of the Mother of Jesus, then, we can see two things: on the one hand, her affectionate concern for people, that maternal affection which makes her aware of the problems of others. We see her heartfelt goodness and her willingness to help. . . . To her we entrust our cares, our needs, and our troubles. Her maternal readiness to help, in which we trust, appears here for the first time in the holy Scriptures.

But in addition to this first aspect, with which we are all familiar, there is another, which we could easily overlook: Mary leaves everything to the Lord's judgment. At Nazareth she gave over her will, immersing it in the will of God: "Here am I, the servant of the Lord; let it be with me according to your word" (Luke 1:38). And this continues to be her fundamental attitude. This is how she teaches us to pray: not by seeking to assert before God our own will and our own desires, however important they may be, however reasonable they might appear to us, but rather to bring them before him and to let him decide what he intends to do. From Mary we learn graciousness and readiness to help, but we also learn humility and generosity in accepting God's will, in the confident conviction that, whatever it may be, it will be our, and my own, true good.

—Homily, September 11, 2006

19. A Double "Yes"
John 2:4

We can understand, I think, very well the attitude and words of Mary, yet we still find it very hard to understand Jesus' answer. In the first place, we don't like the way he addresses her: "Woman." Why doesn't he say: "Mother"? But this title really expresses Mary's place in salvation history. It points to the future, to the hour of the crucifixion, when Jesus will say to her: "Woman, behold your son—Son, behold your mother" (see John 19:26-27). It anticipates the hour when he will make the woman, his mother, the Mother of all his disciples. On the other hand, the title "Woman" recalls the account of the creation of Eve: Adam, surrounded by creation in all its magnificence, experiences loneliness as a human being. Then Eve is created, and in her Adam finds the companion whom he longed for; and he gives her the name "woman." In the Gospel of John, then, Mary represents the new, the definitive woman, the companion of the Redeemer, our Mother: the name, which seemed so lacking in affection, actually expresses the grandeur of Mary's enduring mission.

Yet we like even less what Jesus at Cana then says to Mary: "Woman, what have I to do with you? My hour has not yet come" (John 2:4). We want to object: you have a lot to do with her! It was Mary who gave you flesh and blood, who gave you your body, and not only your body; with the "yes" which rose from the depths of her heart she bore you in her womb, and with a mother's love she gave you life and introduced you to the community of the people of Israel. But if this is how we speak to Jesus, then we are already well along the way toward understanding his answer. Because all this should remind us that at the incarnation of Jesus two dialogues took place; the two go together and blend into one. First, there is Mary's dialogue with the archangel Gabriel, where she says, "Let it be with me according to your word" (Luke 1:38). But there is a text parallel to this, so to speak, within God himself, which we read about in the Letter to the Hebrews, when it says that the words of Psalm 40 became a kind of dialogue between the Father and the Son—a dialogue which set in motion the incarnation. The eternal Son says to the Father: "Sacrifices and offerings you have not desired, but a body you have prepared for me . . . See, I have come to do your will" (Hebrews 10:5-7; see Psalm 40:6-8). The "yes" of the Son: "I have come to do your will," and the "yes" of Mary: "Let it be with me according to your word"—this double "yes" becomes a single "yes," and thus the Word becomes flesh in Mary. In this double "yes" the obedience of the Son is embodied, and by her own "yes" Mary gives him that body. "Woman, what have I to do with you?"

Ultimately, what each has to do with the other is found in this double "yes" which resulted in the incarnation. The Lord's answer points to this point of profound unity. It is precisely to this that he points his mother. Here, in their common "yes" to the will of the Father, an answer is found. We too need to learn always anew how to progress toward this point; there we will find the answer to our questions.

—Homily, September 11, 2006

20. The Wedding Feast of the Lamb
John 2:4-11

Jesus never acts completely alone and never for the sake of pleasing others. The Father is always the starting point of his actions, and this is what unites him to Mary, because she wished to make her request in this same unity of will with the Father. And so, surprisingly, after hearing Jesus' answer ["My hour has not yet come"], which apparently refuses her request, she can simply say to the servants, "Do whatever he tells you" (John 2:5). Jesus is not a wonder-worker; he does not play games with his power in what is, after all, a private affair. No, he gives a sign in which he proclaims his hour, the hour of the wedding feast, the hour of union between God and man. He does not merely "make" wine but transforms the human wedding feast into an image of the divine wedding feast, to which the Father invites us through the Son and in which he gives us every good thing, represented by the abundance of wine. The wedding feast becomes an image of that moment when Jesus pushed love to the utmost, let his body be rent and thus gave himself to us forever, having become completely one with us—a marriage between God and man. The hour of the cross, the hour which is the source of the sacrament, in which he gives himself really to us in flesh and blood, puts his body into our hands and our hearts; this is the hour of the wedding feast. Thus, a momentary need is resolved in a truly divine manner, and the initial request is superabundantly granted. Jesus' hour has not yet arrived, but in the sign of the water changed into wine, in the sign of the festive gift, he even now anticipates that hour.

Jesus' "hour" is the cross; his definitive hour will be his return at the end of time. He continually anticipates also this definitive hour in the Eucharist in which, even now, he always comes to us. And he does this ever anew through the intercession of his mother, through the intercession of the Church, which cries out to him in the Eucharistic prayers: "Come, Lord Jesus!" In the Canon of the Mass, the Church constantly prays for this "hour" to be anticipated, asking that he may come even now and be given to us. And so we want to let ourselves be guided by Mary, . . . by the Mother of all the faithful, toward the "hour" of Jesus. Let us ask him for the gift of a deeper knowledge and understanding of him. And may our reception of him not be reduced to the moment of Communion alone. Jesus remains present in the sacred Host and he awaits us constantly. . . . Mary and Jesus go together. Through Mary we want to continue our conversation with the Lord and to learn how to receive him better. Holy Mother of God, pray for us, just as at Cana you prayed for the bride and the bridegroom! Guide us toward Jesus—ever anew! Amen!

—Homily, September 11, 2006

21. IMITATING JESUS
MATTHEW 5:3-10

Jesus says: Blessed are the poor in spirit, blessed those who mourn, the meek; blessed those who hunger and thirst for justice, the merciful; blessed the pure in heart, the peacemakers, the persecuted for the sake of justice (see Matthew 5:3-10).

In truth, the blessed par excellence is only Jesus. He is, in fact, the true poor in spirit, the one afflicted, the meek one, the one hungering and thirsting for justice, the merciful, the pure of heart, the peacemaker. He is the one persecuted for the sake of justice.

The beatitudes show us the spiritual features of Jesus and thus express his mystery, the mystery of his death and resurrection, of his passion and of the joy of his resurrection. This mystery, which is the mystery of true blessedness, invites us to follow Jesus and thus to walk toward it.

To the extent that we accept his proposal and set out to follow him—each one in his own circumstances—we too can participate in his blessedness. With him, the impossible becomes possible, and even a camel can pass through the eye of a needle (see Mark 10:25); with his help, only with his help, can we become perfect as the heavenly Father is perfect (see Matthew 5:48).

—Homily, November 1, 2006

22. A REVOLUTIONARY LOVE
LUKE 6:27-38

This Sunday's gospel contains some of the most typical and forceful words of Jesus' preaching: "Love your enemies" (Luke 6:27). It is taken from Luke's gospel but is also found in Matthew's (5:44), in the context of the programmatic discourse that opens with the famous "beatitudes." Jesus delivered it in Galilee at the beginning of his public life: it is, as it were, a "manifesto" presented to all, in which he asks for his disciples' adherence, proposing his model of life to them in radical terms.

But what do his words mean? Why does Jesus ask us to love precisely our enemies, that is, a love which exceeds human capacities?

Actually, Christ's proposal is realistic because it takes into account that in the world there is *too much* violence, *too much* injustice, and therefore that this situation cannot be overcome except by countering it with *more* love, with *more* goodness. This *more* comes from God: it is his mercy which was made flesh in Jesus and which alone can "tip the balance" of the world from evil to good, starting with that small and decisive "world" which is the human heart.

This gospel passage is rightly considered the *magna carta* of Christian nonviolence. It does not consist in succumbing to evil, as a false interpretation of "turning the other cheek" (see Luke 6:29) claims, but in responding to evil with good (see Romans 12:17-21) and thereby breaking the chain of injustice.

One then understands that for Christians, nonviolence is not merely tactical behavior but a person's way of being, the attitude of one who *is so convinced of God's love and power* that he is not afraid to tackle evil with the weapons of love and truth alone.

Love of one's enemy constitutes the nucleus of the "Christian revolution," a revolution not based on strategies of economic, political, or media power; . . . a love that does not rely ultimately on human resources but is a gift of God, which is obtained by trusting solely and unreservedly in his merciful goodness. Here is the newness of the gospel which silently changes the world! Here is the heroism of the "lowly" who believe in God's love and spread it, even at the cost of their lives.

Let us ask the Virgin Mary, docile disciple of the Redeemer who helps us to allow ourselves to be won over without reserve by that love, to learn to love as he loved us, to be merciful as our Father in heaven is merciful (see Luke 6:36).

—Angelus, February 18, 2007

23. THIRSTING FOR GOD
JOHN 4:5-42

Through the symbol of water, which we find in the . . . gospel passage on the Samaritan woman, the Word of God transmits to us an ever lively and timely message: God thirsts for our faith and wants us to find the source of our authentic happiness in him. Every believer is in danger of practicing a false religiosity, of not seeking in God the answer to the most intimate expectations of the heart, but on the contrary, treating God as though he were at the service of our desires and projects. . . .

The symbolism of water [appears] with great eloquence in this famous gospel passage that recounts Jesus' meeting with the Samaritan woman in Sychar, by Jacob's well. We immediately perceive a link between the well, built by the great patriarch of Israel to guarantee his family water, and salvation history where God gives humanity water welling up to eternal life. If there is a physical thirst for water that is indispensable for life on this earth, there is also a spiritual thirst in man that God alone can satisfy. This is clearly visible in the dialogue between Jesus and the woman who came to Jacob's well to draw water. Everything begins with Jesus' request: "Give me a drink" (see John 4:5-7). At first sight it seems a simple request for a little water in the hot midday sun. In fact, with this question, addressed moreover to a Samaritan woman—there was bad blood between the Jews and the Samaritans—Jesus triggers in the woman to whom he is talking an inner process that kindles within her the desire for something more profound. St. Augustine comments: "Although Jesus asked for a drink, his real thirst was for this woman's faith (in *Io. Ev.*, Tract 15, 11: *PL* 35, 1514). In fact, at a certain point, it was the woman herself who asked Jesus for the water (see John 4:15), thereby demonstrating that in every person, there is an inherent need for God and for salvation that only God can satisfy. It is a thirst for the infinite which only the water that Jesus offers, the living water of the Spirit, can quench. In a little while, in the Preface [of the Mass], we shall hear these words: Jesus "asked the woman of Samaria for water to drink, and had already prepared for her the gift of faith. In his thirst to receive her faith, he awakened in her heart the fire of your love."

Dear brothers and sisters, in this dialogue between Jesus and the Samaritan woman we see outlined the spiritual itinerary that each one of us, that every Christian community, is ceaselessly called to rediscover and follow. Proclaimed in this Lenten season, this gospel passage acquires a particularly important value for catechumens who are already approaching baptism. This Third Sunday of Lent is in fact linked to the so-called "first scrutiny," which is a sacramental rite of purification and grace. The

Samaritan woman thus becomes the figure of the catechumen enlightened and converted to the faith, who longs for the living water and is purified by the Lord's action and words. Yet we who have already been baptized, but are also still on the way to becoming true Christians, find in this gospel episode an incentive to rediscover the importance and meaning of our Christian life, the true desire of God who lives in us. As he did with the Samaritan woman, Jesus wishes to bring us to powerfully profess our faith in him so that we may then proclaim and witness to our brethren the joy of the encounter with him and the marvels that his love works in our existence. Faith is born from the encounter with Jesus, recognized and accepted as the definitive Revealer and Savior in whom God's face is revealed. Once the Lord has won the Samaritan woman's heart, her life is transformed, and she runs without delay to take the good news to her people (see John 4:29).

—Homily, February 24, 2008

24. A God Who Is Close
John 6:47-69

H e who feeds on my flesh and drinks my blood remains in me, and I in him" (John 6:56). How is it possible not to rejoice in such a promise?

However, we have heard that at his first announcement, instead of rejoicing, the people started to murmur in protest: "How can he give us his flesh to eat?" (John 6:52). To tell the truth, that attitude has frequently been repeated in the course of history. One might say that basically people do not want to have God so close, to be so easily within reach or to share so deeply in the events of their daily life. Rather, people want him to be great and, in brief, we also often want him to be a little distant from us. Questions are then raised that are intended to show that, after all, such closeness would be impossible.

But the words that Christ spoke on that occasion have lost none of their clarity: "Let me solemnly assure you, if you do not eat the flesh of the Son of Man and drink his blood, you have no life in you" (John 6:53). Truly, we need a God who is close to us. In the face of the murmur of protest, Jesus might have fallen back on reassuring words: "Friends," he could have said, "do not worry! I spoke of flesh, but it is only a symbol. What I mean is only a deep communion of sentiments."

But no, Jesus did not have recourse to such soothing words. He stuck to his assertion, to all his realism, even when he saw many of his disciples breaking away (see John 6:66). Indeed, he showed his readiness to accept even desertion by his apostles, while not in any way changing the substance of his discourse: "Do you want to leave me too?" (6:67), he asked. Thanks be to God, Peter's response was one that even we can make our own today with full awareness: "Lord, to whom shall we go? You have the words of eternal life" (6:68). We need a God who is close, a God who puts himself in our hands and who loves us.

Christ is truly present among us in the Eucharist. His presence is not static. It is a dynamic presence that grasps us, to make us his own, to make us assimilate him. Christ draws us to him, he makes us come out of ourselves to make us all one with him. In this way he also integrates us in the communities of brothers and sisters, and communion with the Lord is always also communion with our brothers and sisters. And we see the beauty of this communion that the Blessed Eucharist gives us.

—Homily, May 29, 2005

25. SEEING AND KNOWING JESUS
MATTHEW 16:13-20

Today's feast [Sts. Peter and Paul] offers me the opportunity to meditate once again on Peter's confession, the decisive moment in the journey of the disciples with Jesus. The synoptic gospels have it take place in the district of Caesarea Philippi (see Matthew 16:13-20; Mark 8:27-30; Luke 9:18-22).

John, for his part, keeps for us another important confession by Peter, after the miracle of the multiplication of the loaves and Jesus' address in the synagogue of Capernaum (see John 6:66-70). Matthew, in the text just proclaimed, recalls Jesus' attribution of the nickname *Cephas,* "Rock," to Simon. Jesus said that he desired to build his Church "on this rock" and with this in view, conferred on Peter the power of the keys (Matthew 16:17-19). It clearly emerges from these accounts that Peter's confession is inseparable from his pastoral duty to Christ's flock which was entrusted to him.

According to all the Evangelists, Simon's confession takes place at a crucial moment in Jesus' life when, after preaching in Galilee, he resolutely set out for Jerusalem in order to bring his saving mission to completion with his death on the cross and his resurrection. The disciples were involved in this decision:

Jesus invited them to make a choice that would bring them to distinguish themselves from the crowd so as to become the community of those who believed in him, his "family," the beginning of the Church.

In fact, there are two ways of "seeing" and "knowing" Jesus: one—that of the crowd—is more superficial; the other—that of the disciples—more penetrating and genuine. With his twofold question—"What do the people say?" and "Who do you say that I am?"—Jesus invited the disciples to become aware of this different perspective.

The people thought that Jesus was a prophet. This was not wrong, but it does not suffice; it is inadequate. In fact, it was a matter of delving deep, of recognizing the uniqueness of the person of Jesus of Nazareth and his newness.

This is how it still is today: many people draw near to Jesus, as it were, from the outside. Great scholars recognize his spiritual and moral stature and his influence on human history, comparing him to Buddha, Confucius, Socrates, and other wise and important historical figures.

Yet they do not manage to recognize him in his uniqueness. What Jesus said to Philip at the Last Supper springs to mind: "Have I been with you so long, and yet you do not know me, Philip?" (John 14:9).

Jesus is often also considered as one of the great founders of a religion from which everyone may take something in order to form his or her own conviction. Today, too, "people" have different opinions about Jesus, just as they did then. And as he did then, Jesus also repeats his question to us, his disciples today: "And who do you say that I am?"

Let us make Peter's answer our own. According to the Gospel of Mark, he said: "You are the Christ" (8:29); in Luke, the affirmation is "The Christ of God" (9:20); in Matthew resounds, "You are the Christ, the Son of the living God" (16:16); finally, in John: "You are the Holy One of God" (6:69). These are all correct answers, which are also right for us.

—Homily, June 29, 2007

26. Walk in the Light
Mark 9:2-10

Jesus took Peter, James, and John with him up a high mountain and was transfigured before them, [his garments] becoming so dazzlingly bright that they were "whiter than the work of any bleacher could make them" (Mark 9:2-10). . . .

On the transfigured face of Jesus, a ray of light which he held within shines forth. This same light was to shine on Christ's face on the day of the resurrection. In this sense, the transfiguration appears as a foretaste of the paschal mystery.

The transfiguration invites us to open the eyes of our hearts to the mystery of God's light, present throughout salvation history. At the beginning of creation, the Almighty had already said: "*Fiat lux*—let there be light!" (Genesis 1:3), and the light was separated from the darkness. Like the other created things, light is a sign that reveals something of God: it is, as it were, a reflection of his glory which accompanies its manifestations. When God appears, "His brightness was like the light, rays flashed from his hand" (Habakkuk 3:4).

Light, it is said in the psalms, is the mantle with which God covers himself (see Psalm 104:2). In the Book of Wisdom, the symbolism of light is used to describe the very essence of God:

wisdom, an outpouring of his glory, is "a reflection of eternal light" superior to any created light (see Wisdom 7:26, 29ff).

In the New Testament, it is Christ who constitutes the full manifestation of God's light. His resurrection defeated the power of the darkness of evil forever. With the risen Christ, truth and love triumph over deceit and sin. In him, God's light henceforth illumines definitively human life and the course of history: "I am the light of the world," he says in the gospel; "he who follows me will not walk in darkness, but will have the light of life" (John 8:12).

In our time, too, we urgently need to emerge from the darkness of evil, to experience the joy of the children of light! May Mary . . . obtain this gift for us.

—Angelus, August 6, 2006

27. Prayer: A Matter of Life or Death
Luke 9:28-36

The Evangelist Luke emphasizes that Jesus went up on the mountain *"to pray"* (9:28), together with the apostles Peter, James, and John, and it was *"while he prayed"* (9:29) that the luminous mystery of his transfiguration occurred.

Thus, for the three apostles, going up the mountain meant being involved in the prayer of Jesus, who frequently withdrew in prayer, especially at dawn and after sunset, and sometimes all night. However, this was the only time, on the mountain, that he chose to reveal to his friends the inner light that filled him when he prayed: his face, we read in the gospel, shone and his clothes were radiant with the splendor of the divine Person of the incarnate Word (see Luke 9:29).

There is another detail proper to St. Luke's narrative which deserves emphasis: the mention of the topic of Jesus' conversation with Moses and Elijah, who appeared beside him when he was transfigured. As the Evangelist tells us, they "talked with him . . . and spoke of his departure [in Greek, *éxodos*], which he was to accomplish at Jerusalem" (9:31).

Therefore, Jesus listens to the law and the prophets who spoke to him about his death and resurrection. In his intimate dialogue with the Father, he did not depart from history; he did not flee the mission for which he came into the world, although he knew that to attain glory, he would have to pass through the cross.

On the contrary, Christ enters more deeply into this mission, adhering with all his being to the Father's will; he shows us that true prayer consists precisely in uniting our will with that of God. For a Christian, therefore, to pray is not to evade reality and the responsibilities it brings, but rather to fully assume them, trusting in the faithful and inexhaustible love of the Lord.

For this reason, the verification of the transfiguration is, paradoxically, the agony in Gethsemane (see Luke 22:39-46). With his impending passion, Jesus was to feel mortal anguish and entrust himself to the divine will; his prayer at that moment would become a pledge of salvation for us all.

Indeed, Christ was to implore the heavenly Father "to free him from death," and as the author of the Letter to the Hebrews wrote, "He was heard for his godly fear" (5:7). The resurrection is proof that he was heard.

Dear brothers and sisters, prayer is not an accessory or "optional," but a question of life or death. In fact, only those who pray—in other words, who entrust themselves to God with filial love—can enter eternal life, which is God himself. . . . Let us ask Mary, Mother of the incarnate Word and teacher of the spiritual life, to teach us to pray as her Son did so that our life may be transformed by the light of his presence.

—Angelus, March 4, 2007

28. THE FREEDOM OF OBEDIENCE
LUKE 9:51-62

The Evangelist Luke tells us that "as the time approached when he was to be taken from this world," Jesus "firmly resolved to proceed toward Jerusalem" (Luke 9:51). In the phrase "firmly resolved," we can glimpse Christ's freedom. Indeed, he knows that in Jerusalem, death on a cross awaits him, but in obedience to the Father's will, he offers himself for love. It is in his very obedience to the Father that Jesus achieves his own freedom as a conscious decision motivated by love.

Who is freer than the One who is the Almighty? He did not, however, live his freedom as an arbitrary power or as domination. He lived it as a service. In this way he "filled" freedom with content, which would otherwise have remained an "empty" possibility of doing or not doing something.

Like human life itself, freedom draws its meaning from love. Indeed, who is the freest? Someone who selfishly keeps all possibilities open for fear of losing them, or someone who expends himself "firmly resolved" to serve, and thereby finds himself full of life because of the love he has given and received?

The apostle Paul, writing to the Christians of Galatia (today in Turkey), said, "You were called to freedom, brethren; only do not use your freedom as an opportunity for the flesh, but through love be servants of one another" (Galatians 5:13).

Living according to the flesh means following the selfish tendencies of human nature. Living according to the Spirit, on the other hand, means allowing oneself to be guided in intentions and works by God's love, which Christ has given to us. Therefore, Christian freedom is quite the opposite of arbitrariness; it consists in following Christ in the gift of self even to the sacrifice of the cross.

It may seem a paradox, but the Lord lived the crowning point of his freedom on the cross as a summit of love. When they shouted at him on Calvary, "If you are the Son of God, come down from the cross!" he showed his freedom as the Son precisely by remaining on that scaffold, to do the Father's merciful will to the very end.

Other witnesses to the truth have shared this experience, men and women who showed that they remained free even in a prison cell and under the threat of torture. "The truth will set you free." Those who side with the truth will never be slaves of any power but will always make themselves freely servants of their brothers and sisters.

Let us look at Mary Most Holy. A humble handmaid of the Lord, the Virgin is the model of a spiritual person who is totally free because she is immaculate, immune to sin, and all holy, dedicated to the service of God and neighbor. May she help us with her motherly care to follow Jesus, to know the truth, and to live freedom in love.

—Angelus, July 1, 2007

29. Preparing the Way
Luke 10:1-12, 17-20

The gospel today presents Jesus sending out seventy-two disciples to the villages he is about to visit in order to prepare the way. This is a particular feature of the Evangelist Luke, who stressed that the mission was not exclusive to the twelve apostles but extended also to the other disciples. Indeed, Jesus said: "The harvest is plentiful but the laborers are few" (Luke 10:2). There is work for all in God's field. Christ, however, did not limit himself to sending out his missionaries; he also gave them clear and precise instructions on how to behave. He first sent them out "two by two" so that they might help each other and bear witness to brotherly love. He warned them that they would be like "lambs in the midst of wolves." They were to be peaceful in spite of everything, and were to bear a message of peace in every situation; they were not to take clothes or money with them in order to live on whatever Providence offered them; they were to heal the sick as a sign of God's mercy; wherever people rejected them, they were to depart, doing no more than to alert them to their responsibility for rejecting the kingdom of God. St. Luke highlighted the disciples' enthusiasm at the good results of their mission and recorded Jesus' beautiful expression: "Do not rejoice in this, that the spirits are subject to you; but rejoice that your names are written in heaven" (Luke 10:20). May this gospel reawaken in all the baptized the awareness that they are missionaries of Christ, called to prepare the way for him with words and with the witness of their lives.

—Angelus, July 8, 2007

30. Listen, Obey, Speak
Mark 7:31-37

"He even makes the deaf hear and the mute speak" (Mark 7:37). . . .

Is not being deaf and mute, that is, being unable either to listen or to speak, a sign of a lack of communion and a symptom of division? Division and the inability to communicate, a consequence of sin, are contrary to God's plan. . . . The words "He even makes the deaf hear and the mute speak" are good news that proclaim the coming of the kingdom of God and the healing of the inability to communicate and of division. This message is rediscovered in all of Jesus' preaching and work. Wherever he went, whether traveling through villages, cities, or the countryside, the people "laid the sick in the market places, and besought him that they might touch even the fringe of his garment; and as many as touched it were made well" (Mark 6:56).

The healing of the deaf-mute . . . occurred while Jesus, having left the region of Tyre, was making his way to the Sea of Galilee through the so-called "Decapolis," a multiethnic and multireligious district (see Mark 7:31), an emblematic situation even in our day. As elsewhere, in the Decapolis too, they presented a sick man to Jesus, a man who was deaf and had a speech impediment *(moghìlalon)*, begging Jesus to lay his hands upon him because they considered him a man of God.

Jesus took the man aside from the multitude and performed gestures that infer a salvific contact: he put his fingers into his ears, and touched the tongue of the sick man with his own saliva; then, looking up to heaven, he commanded: "Be opened!" He spoke this command in Aramaic (*Ephphatha*), in all likelihood the language of the people present and of the deaf-mute himself. The Evangelist translated this term into Greek as *dianoìchthēti*. The ears of the deaf man were opened, his tongue was released, and "he spoke plainly" (*orthōs*).

Jesus exhorted them to say nothing about the miracle. But the more he exhorted them, "the more zealously they proclaimed it" (Mark 7:36). And the comment full of wonder of those who had been there recalls the preaching of Isaiah concerning the coming of the Messiah: "He even makes the deaf hear and the mute speak" (7:37).

The first lesson we draw from this biblical episode, also recalled in the Rite of Baptism, is that listening, in the Christian perspective, is a priority.

In this regard, Jesus says explicitly: "Blessed . . . are those who hear the word of God and keep it" (Luke 11:28). Indeed, to Martha, worried about many things, he said that "one thing is needful" (10:42). And from the context it becomes evident that this "one thing" is the obedient listening to the Word. Therefore, listening to the Word of God is a priority for our ecumenical commitment. Indeed, it is not we who act or who organize the unity of the Church. The Church does not make herself or live of herself, but from the creative Word that comes from the mouth of God.

To listen to the word of God together; to practice the *lectio divina* of the Bible, that is, reading linked with prayer; letting ourselves be amazed by the newness of the Word of God that never ages and is never depleted; overcoming our deafness to those words that do not correspond with our prejudices and our opinions; to listen and also to study, in the communion of believers of all ages—all these things constitute a path to be taken in order to achieve unity in the faith as a response to listening to the Word.

Anyone who listens to the Word of God can and must speak and transmit it to others, to those who have never heard it, or who have forgotten it and buried it under the thorny troubles and deceptions of the world (see Matthew 13:22).

We must ask ourselves: Have not we Christians become perhaps too silent? Do we not perhaps lack the courage to speak out and witness as did those who witnessed the healing of the deaf-mute in the Decapolis? Our world needs this witness; above all, it is waiting for the common testimony of Christians.

Therefore, listening to the God who speaks also implies a reciprocal listening, the dialogue between the churches and the ecclesial communities. Honest and loyal dialogue is the typical and indispensable instrument in the quest for unity.

—Homily, January 25, 2007

31. Minding Our Destiny
Luke 12:32-48

The gospel . . . asks Christians to detach themselves from material goods, which are for the most part illusory, and to do their duty faithfully, constantly aspiring to heaven. May the believer remain alert and watchful to be ready to welcome Jesus when he comes in his glory.

By means of examples taken from everyday life, the Lord exhorts his disciples, that is, us, to live with this inner disposition, like those servants in the parable who were waiting for their master's return. "Blessed are those servants," he said, "whom the master finds awake when he comes" (Luke 12:37). We must therefore watch, praying and doing good.

It is true, we are all travelers on earth, as . . . the Letter to the Hebrews appropriately reminds us. It presents Abraham to us in the clothes of a pilgrim, as a nomad who lives in a tent and sojourns in a foreign land. He has faith to guide him. "By faith," the sacred author wrote, "Abraham obeyed when he was called to go out to a place which he was to receive as an inheritance; and he went out, not knowing where he was to go" (Hebrews 11:8). Indeed, Abraham's true destination was "the city which has foundations, whose builder and maker is God" (11:10).

The city to which he was alluding is not in this world but is the heavenly Jerusalem, paradise.

This was well known to the primitive Christian community, which considered itself "alien" here below and called its populated nucleuses in the cities "parishes," which means, precisely, colonies of foreigners [in Greek, *paroikoi*] (see 1 Peter 2:11). In this way, the first Christians expressed the most important characteristic of the Church, which is precisely the tension of living in this life in light of heaven.

. . . The Word, therefore, desires to invite us to think of "the life of the world to come," as we repeat every time we make our profession of faith with the Creed. It is an invitation to spend our life wisely and with foresight, to consider attentively our destiny; in other words, those realities which we call final: death, the last judgment, eternity, hell, and heaven. And it is exactly in this way that we assume responsibility for the world and build a better world.

May the Virgin Mary, who watches over us from heaven, help us not to forget that here on earth we are only passing through, and may she teach us to prepare ourselves to encounter Jesus, who is "seated at the right hand of the Father. He will come again in glory to judge the living and the dead."

—Angelus, August 12, 2007

32. THE MOST EFFECTIVE RESPONSE TO EVIL
LUKE 13:1-9

Th[is] passage of Luke's gospel . . . relates Jesus' comments on two events of his time. The first: the uprising of some Galileans, which Pilate repressed with bloodshed. The second: the fall of the tower of Jerusalem, which claimed eighteen victims. Two very distinct, tragic events: one caused by man, the other accidental.

According to the mentality of the time, people were inclined to think that the disgrace which struck the victims was due to some grave fault of their own. Jesus instead says, "Do you think that these Galileans were worse sinners than all the other Galileans. . . . Or those eighteen upon whom the tower in Siloam fell and killed them, do you think that they were worse offenders than all the others who dwelt in Jerusalem?" (Luke 13:2, 4). And in both cases he concludes: "I tell you, No; but unless you repent you will all likewise perish" (13:3, 5).

This, then, is the point to which Jesus wants to bring his listeners: the necessity for conversion. He does not propose it in legalistic terms, but rather in realistic ones, as the only adequate response to the events that place human certainties in crisis. In the face of certain disgraces, he warns, it does no good to blame the victims. Rather, true wisdom allows one to question the precariousness of existence and to acquire an attitude of responsibility: to do penance and to improve our lives.

This is wisdom; this is the most effective response to evil on every level—interpersonal, social, and international. Christ invites us to respond to evil, first of all, with a serious examination of conscience and the commitment to purify our lives. Otherwise, he says, we will perish; we will all perish in the same way.

In effect, people and societies that live without ever questioning themselves have ruin as their only final destination. Conversion, on the other hand, while not preserving one from problems and misfortunes, allows one to face them in a different "way."

First of all, it helps to prevent evil, disengaging some of its threats. And in any case, it allows one to overcome evil with good: if not always on a factual level, which sometimes is independent of our will, certainly on a spiritual level. In summary: *conversion overcomes the root of evil, which is sin, even if it cannot always avoid its consequences.*

Let us pray to Mary Most Holy, . . . so that she may help every Christian to rediscover the greatness, I would say, the beauty, of conversion. May she help us understand that doing penance and correcting one's conduct is not simply moralism, but the most effective way to change oneself and society for the better.

An adage expresses it well: to light a candle is worth more than to curse the darkness.

—Angelus, March 11, 2007

33. THINKING WITH CHRIST
LUKE 14:15-24

Those who were invited first declined; they did not come.

God's hall remains empty, the banquet seemed to have been prepared in vain. This is what Jesus experienced in the last stages of his activity: official groups, the authorities, say "no" to God's invitation, which is he himself. They do not come. His message, his call, ends in the human "no." However, . . . the empty hall becomes an opportunity to invite a larger number of people. God's love, God's invitation, is extended. Luke recounts this in two episodes. First, the invitation is addressed to the poor, the abandoned, those who were never invited by anyone in the city. . . . God now does what he told the Pharisee to do: he invites those who possess nothing, who are truly hungry, who cannot invite him back, who cannot give him anything.

The second episode follows. He departs from the city to go on the country roads: the homeless are invited. . . . Those who do not at all belong to God, who are outside, are now invited to fill the hall. And Luke, who has handed down this gospel to us, certainly saw in anticipation, in a figurative way, the events recounted later in Acts, where precisely this happens. . . .

Today, too, he will find new ways to call men, and he wants to have us with him as his messengers and servants.

Precisely in our time we know very well how those who were invited first say "no." Indeed, Western Christianity, the new "first guests," now largely excuse themselves; they do not have time to come to the Lord. We know the churches that are ever more empty, seminaries that continue to be empty, religious houses that are increasingly empty; we are familiar with all the forms in which this "No, I have other important things to do" is presented. And it distresses and upsets us to be witnesses of these excuses and refusals of the first guests, who in reality should know the importance of the invitation and should feel drawn in that direction.

What should we do?

First of all, we should ask ourselves: Why is this happening?

In his parable the Lord mentions two reasons: possessions and human relations, which involve people to the extent that they no longer feel the need for anything else to fill their time and therefore their interior existence. . . .

I hold that the first thing to do is what the Lord tells us today in the first reading, and which St. Paul cries to us in God's name: "Your attitude must be Christ's—*Touto phroneite en hymin ho kai en Christo Iesou.*"

Learn to think as Christ thought, learn to think with him! And this thinking is not only the thinking of the mind but also a thinking of the heart.

We learn Jesus Christ's sentiments when we learn to think with him and thus, when we learn to think also of his failure, of his passage through failure, and of the growth of his love in failure.

If we enter into these sentiments of his, if we begin to practice thinking like him and with him, then joy for God is awakened within us, confident that he is the strongest; yes, we can say that love for him is reawakened within us. We feel how beautiful it is that he is there and that we can know him—that we know him in the face of Jesus Christ who suffered for us.

I think this is the first thing: that we ourselves enter into vital contact with God—with the Lord Jesus, the living God; that in us the organ directed to God be strengthened; that we bear within us a perception of his "exquisiteness."

This also gives life to our work, but we also run a risk: one can do much, many things in the ecclesiastical field, all for God . . . and yet remain totally taken up with oneself, without encountering God. Work replaces faith, but then one becomes empty within.

I therefore believe that we must make an effort, above all, to listen to the Lord in prayer, in deep interior participation in the sacraments, in learning the sentiments of God in the faces and the suffering of others, in order to be infected by his joy, his zeal, and his love, and to look at the world with him and starting from him.

If we can succeed in doing this, even in the midst of the many "noes," we will once again find people waiting for him who may perhaps often be odd—the parable clearly says so—but who are nevertheless called to enter his hall.

—Homily, November 7, 2006

34. Feed the Hungry
Luke 16:19-31

Luke's gospel presents to us the parable of the rich man and poor Lazarus. . . . The rich man personifies the wicked use of riches by those who spend them on uncontrolled and selfish luxuries, thinking solely of satisfying themselves without caring at all for the beggar at their door. The poor man, on the contrary, represents the person whom God alone cares for: unlike the rich man he has a name, "Lazarus," an abbreviation of "Eleazarus," which means, precisely, "God helps him."

God does not forget those who are forgotten by all; those who are worthless in human eyes are precious in the Lord's. The story shows how earthly wickedness is overturned by divine justice: after his death, Lazarus was received "in the bosom of Abraham," that is, into eternal bliss, whereas the rich man ended up "in Hades, in torment." This is a new and definitive state of affairs against which no appeal can be made, which is why one must mend one's ways during one's life; to do so after serves no purpose.

This parable can also be interpreted in a social perspective. Pope Paul VI's interpretation of it forty years ago in his encyclical *Populorum progressio* remains unforgettable. Speaking of the campaign against hunger, he wrote, "It is a question . . . of building a world where every man . . . can live a fully human life, . . . where the poor man Lazarus can sit down at the same table with the rich man" (47).

The cause of the numerous situations of destitution, the encyclical recalls, is on the one hand, "servitude imposed . . . by other men," and on the other, "natural forces over which [the person] has not sufficient control" (PP, 47).

Unfortunately, some populations suffer from both these factors. How can we fail to think, at this time especially, of the countries of sub-Saharan Africa, affected by serious floods in the past few days? Nor can we forget the many other humanitarian emergencies in various regions of the planet, in which conflicts for political and economic power contribute to exacerbating existing oppressive environmental situations.

The appeal voiced by Paul VI at that time, "Today the peoples in hunger are making a dramatic appeal to the peoples blessed with abundance" (PP, 3), is still equally pressing today.

We cannot say that we do not know which way to take: we have the law and the prophets, Jesus tells us in the gospel. Those who do not wish to listen to them would not change even if one of the dead were to return to admonish them.

May the Virgin Mary help us to make the most of the present time to listen to and put into practice these words of God. May . . . we become more attentive to our brethren in need, to share with them the much or the little that we have, and to contribute, starting with ourselves, to spreading the logic and style of authentic solidarity.

—Angelus, September 30, 2007

35. Inner Healing
Luke 17:11-19

This . . . gospel presents Jesus healing ten lepers, of whom only one, a Samaritan and therefore a foreigner, returned to thank him. The Lord said to him, "Rise and go your way; your faith has made you well" (Luke 17:19). This gospel passage invites us to a twofold reflection. It first evokes two levels of healing: one, more superficial, concerns the body. The other deeper level touches the innermost depths of the person, what the Bible calls "the heart," and from there spreads to the whole of a person's life. Complete and radical healing is "salvation." By making a distinction between "health" and "salvation," even ordinary language helps us to understand that salvation is far more than health: indeed, it is new, full, and definitive life. Furthermore, Jesus here, as in other circumstances, says the words "Your faith has made you whole." It is faith that saves human beings, reestablishing them in their profound relationship with God, themselves and others; and faith is expressed in gratitude. Those who, like the healed Samaritan, know how to say "thank you" show that they do not consider everything as their due but as a gift that comes ultimately from God, even when it arrives through men and women or through nature. Faith thus entails the opening of the person to the Lord's grace;

it means recognizing that everything is a gift, everything is grace. What a treasure is hidden in two small words: "thank you"!

Jesus healed ten people sick with leprosy, a disease in those times considered a "contagious impurity" that required ritual cleansing (see Leviticus 14:1-37). Indeed, the "leprosy" that truly disfigures the human being and society is sin; it is pride and selfishness that spawn indifference, hatred, and violence in the human soul. No one, save God who is Love, can heal this leprosy of the spirit, which scars the face of humanity. By opening his heart to God, the person who converts is inwardly healed from evil.

–Angelus, October 14, 2007

36. The Logic of Christianity
Mark 9:30-37

In this . . . gospel, for the second time, Jesus proclaims his passion, death, and resurrection to the disciples (Mark 9:30-31). The Evangelist Mark highlights the strong contrast between his mind-set and that of the twelve apostles, who not only do not understand the Teacher's words and clearly reject the idea that he is doomed to encounter death (see 8:32), but also discuss which of them is to be considered "the greatest" (9:34).

Jesus patiently explains his logic to them, the logic of love that makes itself service to the point of the gift of self: "If anyone would be first, he must be last of all and servant of all" (Mark 9:35).

This is the logic of Christianity, which responds to the truth about man created in the image of God, but at the same time contrasts with human selfishness, a consequence of original sin. Every human person is attracted by love—which ultimately is God himself—but often errs in the concrete ways of loving; thus, an originally positive tendency but one polluted by sin can give rise to evil intentions and actions.

. . . This is also recalled in the Letter of St. James: "Wherever jealousy and selfish ambition exist, there will be disorder and every vile practice. But the wisdom from above is first pure, then peaceable, gentle, open to reason, full of mercy and good fruits, without uncertainty or insincerity." And the apostle concludes: "The harvest of righteousness is sown in peace by those who make peace" (James 3:16-18).

These words call to mind the witness of so many Christians who humbly and silently spend their lives serving others for the sake of the Lord Jesus, behaving in practice as servants of love, and hence, "artisans" of peace.

Sometimes certain people are asked for the supreme testimony of blood, which also happened a few days ago to the Italian religious Sr. Leonella Sgorbati, who died as a victim of violence. This sister, who served the poor and the lowly in Somalia for many years, died with the words "I forgive" on her lips. This is the most genuine Christian witness, a peaceful sign of contradiction that demonstrates the victory of love over hatred and evil.

There is no doubt that following Christ is difficult, but as he says, only those who lose their life for his sake and the gospel's will save it (see Mark 8:35), giving full meaning to their existence. There is no other way of being his disciples, there is no other way of witnessing to his love and striving for gospel perfection. May Mary, whom we call upon today as Our Lady of Mercy, open our hearts ever wider to the love of God, a mystery of joy and holiness.

—Angelus, September 24, 2006

37. THE WITNESS OF CHRISTIAN FAMILIES
MARK 10:2-16

The gospel presents to us Jesus' words on marriage. He answered those who asked him whether it was lawful for a man to divorce his wife, as provided by a decree in Mosaic law (see Deuteronomy 24:1), that this was a concession made to Moses because of man's "hardness of heart," whereas the truth about marriage dated back to "the beginning of creation" when, as is written of God in the Book of Genesis, "male and female he created them; for this reason a man shall leave his father and mother and be joined to his wife, and the two shall become one" (Mark 10:6-7; see Genesis 1:27; 2:24).

And Jesus added: "So they are no longer two but one. What therefore God has joined together, let not man put asunder" (Mark 10:8-9). This is God's original plan, as the Second Vatican Council also recalled in the constitution *Gaudium et spes*: "The intimate partnership of life and love which constitutes the married state has been established by the Creator and endowed by him with its own proper laws: it is rooted in the contract of its partners. . . . God himself is the author of marriage" (48).

My thoughts now go to all Christian spouses: I thank the Lord with them for the gift of the Sacrament of Marriage, and I urge them to remain faithful to their vocation in every season of life, "in good times and in bad, in sickness and in health," as they promised in the sacramental rite.

Conscious of the grace they have received, may Christian husbands and wives build a family open to life and capable of facing united the many complex challenges of our time.

Today there is a special need for their witness. There is a need for families that do not let themselves be swept away by modern cultural currents inspired by hedonism and relativism, and who are ready instead to carry out their mission in the Church and in society with generous dedication.

In the apostolic exhortation *Familiaris consortio*, the Servant of God John Paul II wrote that "the sacrament of marriage makes Christian couples and parents witnesses of Christ 'to the end of the earth,' missionaries, in the true and proper sense, of love and life" (54). Their mission is directed both to inside the family—especially in reciprocal service and the education of the children—and to outside it. Indeed, the domestic community is called to be a sign of God's love for all.

The Christian family can only fulfill this mission if it is supported by divine grace. It is therefore necessary for Christian couples to pray tirelessly and to persevere in their daily efforts to maintain the commitments they assumed on their wedding day.

I invoke upon all families, especially those in difficulty, the motherly protection of Our Lady and of her husband, Joseph. Mary, Queen of the family, pray for us!

—Angelus, October 8, 2006

38. FOLLOWING JESUS ON THE WAY
MARK 10:46-52

While the Lord passed through the streets of Jericho, a blind man called Bartimaeus cried out loudly to him: "Jesus, Son of David, have mercy on me!" (Mark 10:48). This prayer moved the heart of Jesus, who stopped, had him called over, and healed him.

The decisive moment was the direct, personal encounter between the Lord and that suffering man. They found each other face-to-face: God with his desire to heal and the man with his desire to be healed; two freedoms, two converging desires. "What do you want me to do for you?" the Lord asks him. "Master, let me receive my sight," the blind man answers. "Go your way, your faith has saved you" (Mark 10:51-52).

With these words, the miracle was worked: God's joy and the man's joy. And Bartimaeus, who had come into the light, as the gospel narrates, "followed him on the way"; that is, he became a disciple of the Lord and went up to Jerusalem with the Master to take part with him in the great mystery of salvation. This account, in the essentiality of its passages, recalls the catechumen's journey toward the Sacrament of Baptism, which in the ancient Church was also known as "Illumination."

Faith is a journey of illumination: it starts with the humility of recognizing oneself as needy of salvation and arrives at the personal encounter with Christ, who calls one to follow him on the way of love. On this model the Church has formulated the itinerary of Christian initiation to prepare for baptism, confirmation (or chrism), and the Eucharist.

In places evangelized of old, where the baptism of children is widespread, young people and adults are offered catechetical and spiritual experiences that enable them to follow the path of a mature and conscious rediscovery of faith in order to then take on a consistent commitment to witness to it.

How important is the work that pastors and catechists do in this field! The rediscovery of the value of one's own baptism is at the root of every Christian's missionary commitment, because as we see in the gospel, those who allow themselves to be fascinated by Christ cannot fail to witness to the joy of following in his footsteps. . . . It is precisely in virtue of baptism that we possess a co-natural missionary vocation.

Let us invoke the intercession of the Virgin Mary so that missionaries of the gospel may multiply. May every baptized person, closely united to the Lord, feel that he is called to proclaim God's love to everyone with the witness of his own life.

—Angelus, October 29, 2006

39. UNEXPECTED GRACE
LUKE 19:1-10

Who was Zacchaeus? A rich man who was a "publican" by profession, that is, a tax collector for the Roman authorities, hence, viewed as a public sinner. Having heard that Jesus would be passing through Jericho, the man was consumed by a great desire to see him, and because he was small of stature, he climbed up into a tree. Jesus stopped exactly under that tree and addressed him by name: "Zacchaeus, make haste and come down; for I must stay at your house today" (Luke 19:5). What a message this simple sentence contains! "Zacchaeus": Jesus called by name a man despised by all. "Today": yes, this very moment was the moment of his salvation. "I must stay": why "I must"? Because the Father, rich in mercy, wants Jesus "to seek and to save the lost" (19:10). The grace of that unexpected meeting was such that it completely changed Zacchaeus' life: "Behold, Lord, the half of my goods I give to the poor; and if I have defrauded anyone of anything, I restore it fourfold" (19:8). Once again, the gospel tells us that love, born in God's heart and working through man's heart, is the power that renews the world.

—Angelus, November 4, 2007

40. DIVINE MERCY
JOHN 8:1-11

The gospel passage recounts the episode of the adulterous woman in two vivid scenes. In the first, we witness a dispute between Jesus and the scribes and Pharisees concerning a woman caught in flagrant adultery who, in accordance with the prescriptions of the Book of Leviticus (see 20:10), was condemned to stoning. In the second scene, a brief but moving dialogue develops between Jesus and the sinner-woman. The pitiless accusers of the woman, citing the law of Moses, provoke Jesus—they call him "Teacher" (*Didáskale*)—asking him whether it would be right to stone her. They were aware of his mercy and his love for sinners and were curious to see how he would manage in such a case which, according to Mosaic law, was crystal clear. But Jesus immediately took the side of the woman. In the first place, he wrote mysterious words on the ground, which the Evangelist does not reveal but which impressed him, and Jesus then spoke the sentence that was to become famous: "Let him who is without sin among you [he uses the term *anamártetos* here, which is the only time it appears in the New Testament] be the first to throw a stone at her" (John 8:7) and begin the stoning. St. Augustine noted, commenting on John's gospel, that "the Lord, in his response, neither failed to respect the law nor departed from his meekness." And Augustine added that with these words, Jesus obliged the accusers to look into themselves, to examine themselves to see whether they too were sinners. Thus, "pierced through as if by a dart as big as a beam, one after another, they all withdrew" (in *Io. Ev.,* Tract 33, 5).

So it was, therefore, that the accusers who had wished to provoke Jesus went away one by one, "beginning with the eldest to the last." When they had all left, the divine Teacher remained alone with the woman. St. Augustine's comment is concise and effective: "*relicti sunt duo: misera et Misericordia,* the two were left alone, the wretched woman and Mercy" (33, 5). Let us pause, dear brothers and sisters, to contemplate this scene where the wretchedness of man and Divine Mercy come face to face, a woman accused of a grave sin and the One who, although he was sinless, burdened himself with our sins, the sins of the whole world. The One who had bent down to write in the dust now raised his eyes and met those of the woman. He did not ask for explanations. Is it not ironic when he asked the woman, "Woman, where are they? Has no one condemned you?" (John 8:10). And his reply was overwhelming: "Neither do I condemn you; go, and do not sin again" (8:11). Again, St. Augustine in his commentary observed: "The Lord did also condemn, but condemned sins, not man. For if he were a patron of sin, he would say, 'Neither will I condemn you; go, live as you will; be secure in my deliverance; however much you sin, I will deliver you from all punishment.' He said not this" (33, 6).

Dear friends, from the Word of God we have just heard emerge practical instructions for our life. Jesus does not enter into a theoretical discussion with his interlocutors . . . , but his goal is to save a soul and reveal that salvation is only found in God's love. This is why he came down to the earth; this is why he was to die on the cross and why the Father was to raise him on the third day. Jesus came to tell us that he wants us all in paradise and that hell, about which little is said in our time, exists and is eternal for those who close their hearts to his love. In this episode too, therefore, we understand that our real enemy is attachment to sin, which can lead us to failure in our lives. Jesus sent the adulterous woman away with this recommendation: "Go, and do not sin again." He forgives her so that "from now on" she will sin no more. In a similar episode, that of the repentant woman, a former sinner whom we come across in Luke's gospel (see 7:36-50), he welcomed a woman who had repented and sent her peacefully on her way. Here, instead, the adulterous woman simply receives an unconditional pardon. In both cases—for the repentant woman sinner and for the adulterous woman—the message is the same. In one case it is stressed that there is no forgiveness without the desire for forgiveness, without opening the heart to forgiveness; here it is highlighted that only divine forgiveness and divine love received with an open and sincere heart give us the strength to resist evil and "to sin no more," to let ourselves be struck by God's love so that it becomes our strength. Jesus' attitude thus becomes a model to follow for every community, which is called to make love and forgiveness the vibrant heart of its life.

—Homily, March 25, 2007

41. SPIRITUAL BLINDNESS
JOHN 9:1-41

Let us reflect briefly on the account of the man born blind. . . . According to the common mentality of the time, the disciples take it for granted that his blindness was the result of a sin committed by him or his parents. Jesus, however, rejects this prejudice and says, "It was not that this man sinned, or his parents, but that the works of God might be made manifest in him" (John 9:3).

What comfort these words offer us! They let us hear the living voice of God, who is provident and wise Love! In the face of men and women marked by limitations and suffering, Jesus did not think of their possible guilt but rather of the will of God who created man for life. And so he solemnly declares: "We must work the works of him who sent me. . . . As long as I am in the world, I am the light of the world" (John 9:5).

And he immediately takes action: mixing a little earth with saliva he made mud and spread it on the eyes of the blind man. This act alludes to the creation of man, which the Bible recounts using the symbol of dust from the ground, fashioned and enlivened by God's breath (Genesis 2:7). In fact, "Adam" means "ground," and the human body was in effect formed of particles of soil. By healing the blind man, Jesus worked a new creation.

But this healing sparked heated debate because Jesus did it on the Sabbath, thereby in the Pharisees' opinion, violating the feast day precept. Thus, at the end of the account, Jesus and the blind man are both cast out, the former because he broke the law and the latter because, despite being healed, he remained marked as a sinner from birth.

Jesus reveals to the blind man whom he had healed that he had come into the world for judgment, to separate the blind who can be healed from those who do not allow themselves to be healed because they consider themselves healthy. Indeed, the temptation to build himself an ideological security system is strong in man; even religion can become an element of this system, as can atheism or secularism, but in letting this happen, one is blinded by one's own selfishness.

Dear brothers and sisters, let us allow ourselves to be healed by Jesus, who can and wants to give us God's light! Let us confess our blindness, our shortsightedness, and especially what the Bible calls the "great transgression" (see Psalm 19:13): pride. May Mary Most Holy, who by conceiving Christ in the flesh gave the world the true light, help us to do this.

—Angelus, March 2, 2008

42. AWAKENED FROM DEATH
JOHN 11:1-45

The gospel of the resurrection of Lazarus . . . concerns the last "sign" fulfilled by Jesus, after which the chief priests convened the Sanhedrin and deliberated killing him, and decided to kill the same Lazarus who was living proof of the divinity of Christ, the Lord of life and death. Actually, this gospel passage shows Jesus as true Man and true God. First of all, the Evangelist insists on his friendship with Lazarus and his sisters, Martha and Mary. He emphasizes that "Jesus loved" them (John 11:5), and this is why he wanted to accomplish the great wonder. "Our friend Lazarus has fallen asleep, but I go to awaken him out of sleep" (11:11), he tells his disciples, expressing God's viewpoint on physical death with the metaphor of sleep. God sees it exactly as sleep, from which he can awaken us. Jesus has shown an absolute power regarding this death, seen when he gives life back to the widow of Nain's young son (see Luke 7:11-17) and to the twelve-year-old girl (see Mark 5:35-43). Precisely concerning her, he said, "The child is not dead but sleeping" (5:39), attracting the derision of those present. But in truth it is exactly like this: bodily death is a sleep from which God can awaken us at any moment.

This lordship over death does not impede Jesus from feeling sincere "com-passion" for the sorrow of detachment. Seeing Martha and Mary and those who had come to console them weeping, Jesus "was deeply moved in spirit and troubled," and lastly, "wept" (John 11:33, 35). Christ's heart is divine-human: in him God and man meet perfectly, without separation and without confusion. He is the image, or rather, the incarnation of God who is love, mercy, paternal and maternal tenderness, of God who is Life. Therefore, he solemnly declared to Martha: "I am the resurrection and the life; he who believes in me, though he die, yet shall he live, and whoever lives and believes in me shall never die." And he adds, "Do you believe this?" (11:25-26). It is a question that Jesus addresses to each one of us: a question that certainly rises above us, rises above our capacity to understand, and it asks us to entrust ourselves to him as he entrusted himself to the Father. Martha's response is exemplary: "Yes, Lord; I believe that you are the Christ, the Son of God, he who is coming into the world" (11:27). Yes, O Lord! We also believe, notwithstanding our doubts and darkness; we believe in you because you have the words of eternal life. We want to believe in you, who give us a trustworthy hope of life beyond life, of authentic and full life in your kingdom of light and peace.

We entrust this prayer to Mary Most Holy. May her intercession strengthen our faith and hope in Jesus, especially in moments of greater trial and difficulty.

—Angelus, March 9, 2008

43. No Fear
Luke 21:5-19

St. Luke re-proposes the biblical view of history for our reflection and refers to Jesus' words that invite the disciples not to fear, but to face difficulties, misunderstandings, and even persecutions with trust, persevering through faith in him. The Lord says: "When you hear of wars and tumults, do not be terrified; for this must first take place, but the end will not be at once" (Luke 21:9). Keeping this admonition in mind, from the beginning the Church lives in prayerful waiting for her Lord, scrutinizing the signs of the times and putting the faithful on guard against recurring messiahs, who from time to time announce the world's end as imminent. In reality, history must run its course, which brings with it also human dramas and natural calamities. In it a design of salvation is developed that Christ has already brought to fulfillment in his incarnation, death, and resurrection. The Church continues to proclaim this mystery and to announce and accomplish it with her preaching, celebration of the sacraments, and witness of charity.

Dear brothers and sisters, let us welcome Christ's invitation to face daily events by trusting in his providential love. Let us not fear the future, even when it can appear with bleak colors, because the God of Jesus Christ, who entered history to open it to its transcendent fulfillment, is the alpha and the omega, the first and the last (see Revelation 1:8). He guarantees that in every little but genuine act of love, there is the entire sense of the universe, and that the one who does not hesitate to lose his own life for him finds it again in fullness (see Matthew 16:25). . . .

May Mary, Mother of the incarnate Word, accompany us on our earthly pilgrimage. We ask her to sustain the witness of all Christians, so that it is always based on a solid and persevering faith.

—Angelus, November 18, 2007

44. God's Basin
John 13:1-5

Having loved his own who were in the world, he loved them to the end" (John 13:1). God loves his creature, man; he even loves him in his fall and does not leave him to himself. He loves him to the end. He is impelled with his love to the very end, to the extreme: he came down from his divine glory.

He cast aside the raiment of his divine glory and put on the garb of a slave. He came down to the extreme lowliness of our fall. He kneels before us and carries out for us the service of a slave: he washes our dirty feet so that we might be admitted to God's banquet and be made worthy to take our place at his table—something that on our own, we neither could nor would ever be able to do.

God is not a remote God, too distant or too great to be bothered with our trifles. Since God is great, he can also be concerned with small things. Since he is great, the soul of man, the same man, created through eternal love, is not a small thing but great, and worthy of God's love.

God's holiness is not merely an incandescent power before which we are obliged to withdraw, terrified. It is a power of love and therefore a purifying and healing power.

117

God descends and becomes a slave; he washes our feet so that we may come to his table. In this, the entire mystery of Jesus Christ is expressed. In this, what redemption means becomes visible.

The basin in which he washes us is his love, ready to face death. Only love has that purifying power which washes the grime from us and elevates us to God's heights. The basin that purifies us is God himself, who gives himself to us without reserve—to the very depths of his suffering and his death. He is ceaselessly this love that cleanses us; in the sacraments of purification—Baptism and the Sacrament of Penance—he is continually on his knees at our feet and carries out for us the service of a slave, the service of purification, making us capable of God. His love is inexhaustible; it truly goes to the very end.

—Homily, April 13, 2006

45. THE GIFT OF PURIFICATION
JOHN 13:6-11

Y*ou are clean, but not all of you,"* the Lord says (John 13:10). This sentence reveals the great gift of purification that he offers to us because he wants to be at table together with us, to become our food. *"But not all of you"—* the obscure mystery of rejection exists, which becomes apparent with Judas' act, and precisely on Holy Thursday, the day on which Jesus made the gift of himself, it should give us food for thought. The Lord's love knows no bounds, but man can put a limit on it.

"You are clean, but not all of you": What is it that makes man unclean?

It is the rejection of love, not wanting to be loved, not loving. It is pride that believes it has no need of any purification, that is closed to God's saving goodness. It is pride that does not want to admit or recognize that we are in need of purification.

In Judas we see the nature of this rejection even more clearly. He evaluated Jesus in accordance with the criteria of power and success. For him, power and success alone were real; love did not count. And he was greedy: money was more important than communion with Jesus, more important than God and his love.

He thus also became a liar who played a double game and broke with the truth; one who lived in deceit and so lost his sense of the supreme truth, of God. In this way, he became hard of heart and incapable of conversion, of the trusting return of the prodigal son, and he disposed of the life destroyed.

"*You are clean, but not all of you.*" Today the Lord alerts us to the self-sufficiency that puts a limit on his unlimited love. He invites us to imitate his humility, to entrust ourselves to it, to let ourselves be "infected" by it.

He invites us—however lost we may feel—to return home, to let his purifying goodness uplift us and enable us to sit at table with him, with God himself.

—Homily, April 13, 2006

46. Forgiving Tirelessly
John 13:12-15

Let us add a final word to this inexhaustible gospel passage: *"For I have given you an example"* (John 13:15); *"You also ought to wash one another's feet"* (13:14). Of what does "washing one another's feet" consist? What does it actually mean?

This: every good work for others—especially for the suffering and those not considered to be worth much—is a service of the washing of feet.

The Lord calls us to do this: to come down, learn humility and the courage of goodness, and also the readiness to accept rejection and yet to trust in goodness and persevere in it.

But there is another, deeper dimension. The Lord removes the dirt from us with the purifying power of his goodness. Washing one another's feet means, above all, tirelessly forgiving one another, beginning together ever anew, however pointless it may seem. It means purifying one another by bearing with one another and by being tolerant of others; purifying one another, giving one another the sanctifying power of the Word of God, and introducing one another into the sacrament of divine love.

The Lord purifies us, and for this reason, we dare to approach his table. Let us pray to him to give to all of us the grace of being able to one day be guests forever at the eternal nuptial banquet. Amen!

—Homily, April 13, 2006

47. A Love Stronger than Death
John 14:1-31

In his farewell discourse, Jesus announced his imminent death and resurrection to his disciples with these mysterious words: "I go away, and I will come to you," he said (John 14:28). Dying is a "going away." Even if the body of the deceased remains behind, he himself has gone away into the unknown, and we cannot follow him (see 13:36). Yet in Jesus' case, there is something utterly new, which changes the world. In the case of our own death, the "going away" is definitive; there is no return. Jesus, on the other hand, says of his death: "I go away, and I will come to you." It is by going away that he comes. His going ushers in a completely new and greater way of being present. By dying he enters into the love of the Father. His dying is an act of love. Love, however, is immortal. Therefore, his going away is transformed into a new coming, into a form of presence which reaches deeper and does not come to an end. During his earthly life, Jesus, like all of us, was tied to the external conditions of bodily existence: to a determined place and a determined time. Bodiliness places limits on our existence. We cannot be simultaneously in two different places. Our time is destined to come to an end. And between the "I" and the "you," there is a wall of otherness. To be sure, through love we can somehow enter the other's existence. Nevertheless, the insurmountable barrier of being different remains in place. Yet Jesus, who is now totally transformed through the act of love, is free from such barriers and limits. He is able not only to pass through closed doors in the outside world, as the gospels recount (see John 20:19). He can pass through the interior door separating the "I" from the "you," the closed door between yesterday and today, between the past and the future. On the day of his solemn entry into Jerusalem, when some Greeks asked to see him, Jesus replied with the parable of the grain of wheat which has to pass through death in order to bear much fruit. In this way he foretold his own destiny: these words were not addressed simply to one or two Greeks in the space of a few minutes. Through his cross, through his going away, through his dying like the grain of wheat, he would truly arrive among the Greeks, in such a way that they could see him and touch him through faith. His going away is transformed into a coming, in the risen Lord's universal manner of presence, yesterday, today and for ever. He also comes today, and he embraces all times and all places. Now he can even surmount the wall of otherness that separates the "I" from the "you." This happened with Paul, who describes the process of his conversion and his baptism in these words: "It is no longer I who live, but Christ who lives in me" (Galatians 2:20). Through the coming of the risen One, Paul obtained a new identity. His closed "I" was opened. Now he lives in communion with Jesus Christ, in the great "I" of believers who have become—as he puts it—"one in Christ" (3:28).

So, dear friends, it is clear that, through baptism, the mysterious words spoken by Jesus at the Last Supper become present for you once more. In baptism, the Lord enters your life through the door of your heart. We no longer stand alongside or in opposition to one another. He passes through all these doors. This is the reality of baptism: he, the risen One, comes; he comes to you and joins his life with yours, drawing you into the open fire of his love. You become one, one with him, and thus one among yourselves.

At first this can sound rather abstract and unrealistic. But the more you live the life of the baptized, the more you can experience the truth of these words. Believers—the baptized—are never truly cut off from one another. Continents, cultures, social structures, or even historical distances may separate us. But when we meet, we know one another on the basis of the same Lord, the same faith, the same hope, the same love, which form us. Then we experience that the foundation of our lives is the same. We experience that in our inmost depths we are anchored in the same identity, on the basis of which all our outward differences, however great they may be, become secondary. Believers are never totally cut off from one another. We are in communion because of our deepest identity: Christ within us. Thus, faith is a force for peace and reconciliation in the world: distances between people are overcome; in the Lord we have become close (see Ephesians 2:13).

—Homily, March 22, 2008

48. ALL HAS BEEN GIVEN
JOHN 16:12-20

The Lord promises the disciples his Holy Spirit. . . . [who] will guide them to the whole truth. As the living Word of God, Jesus told his disciples everything, and God can give no more than himself. In Jesus, God gave us his whole self, that is, he gave us everything. As well as or together with this, there can be no other revelation which can communicate more or in some way complete the revelation of Christ. In him, in the Son, all has been said to us, all has been given.

But our understanding is limited; thus, the Spirit's mission is to introduce the Church in an ever new way from generation to generation into the greatness of Christ's mystery. The Spirit places nothing different or new beside Christ; no pneumatic revelation comes with the revelation of Christ—as some say—no second level of revelation.

No: "He will have received from me . . . ," Christ says in the gospel (John 16:14). And as Christ says only what he hears and receives from the Father, thus the Holy Spirit is the interpreter of Christ. "He will have received from me." He does not lead us to other places, far from Christ, but takes us further and further into Christ's light. Consequently, Christian revelation is both ever old and new. Thus, all things are and always have been given to us. At the same time, every generation, in the inexhaustible encounter with the Lord—an encounter mediated by the Holy Spirit—always learns something new.

The Holy Spirit, therefore, is the power through which Christ causes us to experience his closeness.

—Homily, May 7, 2005

49. Truth and Love
John 18:33-37

John's gospel presents the dramatic questioning to which Pontius Pilate subjected Jesus when he was handed over to him, accused of usurping the title "King of the Jews."

Jesus answered the Roman governor's questions by declaring that he was a king, but not of this world (see John 18:36). He did not come to rule over peoples and territories but to set people free from the slavery of sin and reconcile them with God. And he added: "For this I was born, and for this I have come into the world, to bear witness to the truth. Everyone who is of the truth hears my voice" (18:37).

But what is the "truth" that Christ came into the world to witness to? The whole of his life reveals that God is love: so this is the truth to which he witnessed to the full with the sacrifice of his own life on Calvary.

The cross is the "throne" where he manifested his sublime kingship as God Love: by offering himself in expiation for the sin of the world, he defeated the "ruler of this world" (John 12:31) and established the kingdom of God once and for all. It is a kingdom that will be fully revealed at the end of time, after the destruction of every enemy and last of all, death (see 1 Corinthians 15:25-26). The Son will then deliver the kingdom to the Father, and God will finally be "everything to everyone" (15:28).

The way to reach this goal is long and admits of no shortcuts; indeed, every person must freely accept the truth of God's love. He is Love and Truth, and neither Love nor Truth are ever imposed: they come knocking at the doors of the heart and the mind, and where they can enter they bring peace and joy. This is how God reigns; this is his project of salvation, a "mystery" in the biblical sense of the word: a plan that is gradually revealed in history.

The Virgin Mary was associated in a very special way with Christ's kingship. God asked her, a humble young woman of Nazareth, to become mother of the Messiah, and Mary responded to this request with her whole self, joining her unconditional "yes" to that of her Son, Jesus, and making herself obedient with him even in his sacrifice. This is why God exalted her above every other creature and Christ crowned her queen of heaven and earth.

Let us entrust the Church and all humanity to her intercession so that God's love can reign in all hearts and his design of justice and peace be fulfilled.

—Angelus, November 26, 2006

50. Contemplating Christ Crucified
John 19:31-37

A verse of John's gospel . . . refers to a messianic prophecy of Zechariah: "*They shall look on him whom they have pierced*" (John 19:37). The beloved disciple, present at Calvary together with Mary, the mother of Jesus, and some other women, was an eyewitness to the thrust of the lance that passed through Christ's side, causing blood and water to flow forth (19:31-34). That gesture by an anonymous Roman soldier, destined to be lost in oblivion, remained impressed on the eyes and heart of the apostle, who takes it up in his gospel. How many conversions have come about down the centuries thanks to the eloquent message of love that the one who looks upon Jesus crucified receives!

In the encyclical letter *Deus Caritas Est*, I wished to emphasize that only by looking at Jesus dead on the cross for us can this fundamental truth be known and contemplated: "God is love" (1 John 4:8, 16). "In this contemplation," I wrote, "the Christian discovers the path along which his life and love must move" (12).

Contemplating the crucified One with the eyes of faith, we can understand in depth what sin is, how tragic is its gravity, and at the same time, how immense is the Lord's power of forgiveness and mercy.

. . . Let us not distance our hearts from this mystery of profound humanity and lofty spirituality. Looking at Christ, we feel at the same time looked at by him. He whom we have pierced with our faults never tires of pouring out upon the world an inexhaustible torrent of merciful love.

May humankind understand that only from this font is it possible to draw the indispensable spiritual energy to build that peace and happiness which every human being continually seeks.

Let us ask the Virgin Mary, pierced in spirit next to the cross of her Son, to obtain for us a solid faith. . . . May she help us to leave all that distances us from listening to Christ and his saving Word.

—Angelus, February 25, 2007

51. Traveling Companions
Luke 24:13-35

The famous account of the disciples of Emmaus . . . tells the tale of two followers of Christ who, on the day after the Sabbath or the third day after his death, were leaving Jerusalem sad and dejected, bound for a village that was not far off called, precisely, Emmaus. They were joined on their way by the risen Jesus, but did not recognize him. Realizing that they were downhearted, he explained, drawing on the Scriptures, that the Messiah had to suffer and die in order to enter into his glory. Then entering the house with them, he sat down to eat, blessed the bread and broke it; and at that instant they recognized him, but he vanished from their sight, leaving them marveling before that broken bread, a new sign of his presence. And they both immediately headed back to Jerusalem to tell the other disciples of the event.

The locality of Emmaus has not been identified with certainty. There are various hypotheses, and this one is not without an evocativeness of its own, for it allows us to think that Emmaus actually represents every place: the road that leads there is the road every Christian, every person, takes. The risen Jesus makes himself our traveling companion as we go on our way, to rekindle the warmth of faith and hope in our hearts and to break the bread of eternal life. In the disciples' conversation with the unknown wayfarer, the words the Evangelist Luke puts in the mouth of one of them are striking: "We had hoped . . ." (Luke 24:21). This verb in the past tense tells all: we believed, we followed, we hoped . . . , but now everything is over. Even Jesus of Nazareth, who had shown himself in his words and actions to be a powerful prophet, has failed, and we are left disappointed.

This drama of the disciples of Emmaus appears like a reflection of the situation of many Christians of our time: it seems that the hope of faith has failed. Faith itself enters a crisis because of negative experiences that make us feel abandoned and betrayed, even by the Lord. But this road to Emmaus on which we walk can become the way of a purification and maturation of our belief in God. Also today we can enter into dialogue with Jesus, listening to his Word. Today, too, he breaks bread for us and gives himself as our Bread. And so the meeting with the risen Christ that is possible even today gives us a deeper and more authentic faith, tempered, so to speak, by the fire of the paschal event; a faith that is robust because it is nourished not by human ideas but by the Word of God and by his Real Presence in the Eucharist.

This marvelous gospel text already contains the structure of holy Mass: in the first part, listening to the Word through the sacred Scriptures; in the second part, the Eucharistic liturgy and communion with Christ present in the Sacrament of his Body and his Blood. In nourishing herself at this twofold table, the Church is constantly built up and renewed from day to day in faith, hope, and charity.

Through the intercession of Mary Most Holy, let us pray that in reliving the experience of the disciples of Emmaus, every Christian and every community may rediscover the grace of the transforming encounter with the risen Lord.

—Regina Coeli, April 6, 2008

52. THE BREATH OF GOD
JOHN 20:19-23

The risen Lord passes through the closed doors and enters the place where the disciples are, and greets them twice with the words: "Peace be with you."

We continually close our doors; we continually want to feel secure and do not want to be disturbed by others and by God. And so, we can continually implore the Lord just for this, that he come to us, overcoming our closure, to bring us his greeting: "Peace be with you."

This greeting of the Lord is a bridge that he builds between heaven and earth. He descends to this bridge, reaching us, and we can climb up on this bridge of peace to reach him. On this bridge, always together with him, we too must reach our neighbor, reach the one who needs us. It is in lowering ourselves, together with Christ, that we rise up to him and up to God. God is Love, and so the descent, the lowering that love demands of us, is at the same time the true ascent. Exactly in this way, lowering ourselves, coming out of ourselves, we reach the dignity of Jesus Christ, the human being's true dignity.

The Lord's greeting of peace is followed by two gestures that are decisive for Pentecost: the Lord wants the disciples to continue his mission: "As the Father has sent me, so I send you" (John 20:21).

After this, he breathes on them and says, "Receive the Holy Spirit. If you forgive men's sins, they are forgiven them; if you hold them bound, they are held bound" (John 20:23). The Lord breathes on the disciples, giving them the Holy Spirit, his own Spirit. The breath of Jesus is the Holy Spirit.

We recognize here, in the first place, an allusion made to the story of creation in the Book of Genesis, where it is written: "The LORD God formed man out of the clay of the ground and blew into his nostrils the breath of life" (Genesis 2:7). Man is this mysterious creature who comes entirely from the earth, but in whom has been placed the breath of God. Jesus breathes on the apostles and gives them the breath of God in a new and greater way.

In people, notwithstanding all of their limitations, there is now something absolutely new: the breath of God. The life of God lives in us—the breath of his love, of his truth, and of his goodness. In this way we can see here, too, an allusion to baptism and confirmation, this new belonging to God that the Lord gives to us. The gospel . . . invites us to this: to live always within the breath of Jesus Christ, receiving life from him, so that he may inspire in us authentic life, the life that no death may ever take away.

—Homily, May 15, 2005

53. Finding Room in God

Acts 1:1-11

What does the Feast of the Ascension of the Lord mean for us? It does not mean that the Lord has departed to some place far from people and from the world. Christ's ascension is not a journey into space toward the most remote stars; for basically, the planets, like the earth, are also made of physical elements.

Christ's ascension means that he no longer belongs to the world of corruption and death that conditions our life. It means that he belongs entirely to God. He, the eternal Son, led our human existence into God's presence, taking with him flesh and blood in a transfigured form.

The human being finds room in God; through Christ, the human being was introduced into the very life of God. And since God embraces and sustains the entire cosmos, the ascension of the Lord means that Christ has not departed from us, but that he is now, thanks to his being with the Father, close to each one of us forever. Each one of us can be on intimate terms with him; each can call upon him. The Lord is always within hearing. We can inwardly draw away from him. We can live turning our backs on him. But he always waits for us and is always close to us.

—Homily, May 7, 2005

54. ONE, HOLY, CATHOLIC, AND APOSTOLIC
ACTS 2:1-12

Fifty days after Easter, the Holy Spirit descended on the community of disciples—who "with one accord devoted themselves to prayer"—gathered with "Mary, the mother of Jesus" and with the twelve apostles (see Acts 1:14; 2:1). We can therefore say that the Church had its solemn beginning with the descent of the Holy Spirit.

In this extraordinary event we find the essential and qualifying characteristics of the Church: the Church is *one,* like the community at Pentecost, who were united in prayer and "concordant": who "were of one heart and soul" (see Acts 4:32).

The Church is *holy,* not by her own merits, but because, animated by the Holy Spirit, she keeps her gaze on Christ, to become conformed to him and to his love.

The Church is *catholic,* because the gospel is destined for all peoples, and for this, already at the beginning, the Holy Spirit made her speak all languages.

The Church is *apostolic,* because, built upon the foundation of the apostles, she faithfully keeps their teaching through the uninterrupted chain of episcopal succession.

What is more, the Church by her nature is *missionary,* and from the day of Pentecost, the Holy Spirit does not cease to move her along the ways of the world to the ends of the earth and to the end of time.

This reality, which we can verify in every epoch, is already anticipated in the Book of Acts, where the gospel passage from the Hebrews to the pagans, from Jerusalem to Rome, is described. Rome represents the pagan world, and hence, all people who are outside of the ancient people of God. Actually, Acts concludes with the arrival of the gospel to Rome.

It can be said, then, that Rome is the concrete name of catholicity and missionary spirit; it expresses fidelity to the origins, to the Church of all times, to a Church that speaks all languages and extends herself to all cultures.

Dear brothers and sisters, the first Pentecost took place when Mary Most Holy was present amid the disciples in the upper room in Jerusalem and prayed. Today, too, let us entrust ourselves to her maternal intercession so that the Holy Spirit may descend in abundance upon the Church in our day, fill the hearts of all the faithful, and enkindle in them the fire of his love.

—Regina Coeli, May 27, 2007

55. Conclusion: Confessing Faith in Christ
1 John 4:7-21

I wish to stress three statements present in this complex and rich text. The central theme of the whole letter appears in verse 15: "Whoever confesses that Jesus is the Son of God, God abides in him, and he in God." Once again John spells out, as he had done before in verses 2 and 3 of chapter 4, the profession of faith, the *confessio*, that ultimately distinguishes us as Christians: faith in the fact that Jesus is the Son of God who has come in the flesh. "No one has ever seen God; the only Son, who is in the bosom of the Father, he has made him known": so we read at the end of the prologue of the fourth gospel (John 1:18). We know who God is through Jesus Christ, the only one who *is* God. It is through him that we come into contact with God. In this time of inter-religious encounters, we are easily tempted to attenuate somewhat this central confession or indeed even to hide it. But by doing this, we do not do a service to encounter or dialogue. We only make God less accessible to others and to ourselves. It is important that we bring to the conversation not fragments but the whole image of God. To be able to do so, our personal communion with Christ and our love of him must grow and deepen. In this common confession and in this common task, there is no division between us. And we pray that this shared foundation will grow ever stronger.

And so we have arrived at the second point which I would like to consider. This is found in verse 14, where we read: "And we have seen and testify that the Father has sent his Son as the Savior of the world." The central word in this sentence is: μαρτυροῦ μεν—we bear witness, we are witnesses. The profession of faith must become witness. The root word μάρτυς brings to mind the fact that a witness of Jesus Christ must affirm by his whole existence, in life and death, the testimony he gives. The author of the letter says of himself: "We have seen" (see 1 John 1:1). Because he has seen, he can be a witness. This presupposes that we also—succeeding generations—are capable of seeing and can bear witness as people who have seen. Let us pray to the Lord that we may see! Let us help one another to develop this capacity so that we can assist the people of our time to see, so that they, in turn, through the world fashioned by themselves, will discover God! Across all the historical barriers may they perceive Jesus anew, the Son sent by God, in whom we see the Father.

In verse 4:9, it is written that God has sent his Son into the world so that we might have life. Is it not the case today that only through an encounter with Jesus Christ can life become really life? To be a witness of Jesus Christ means above all to bear witness to a certain way of living. In a world full of confusion, we must again bear witness to the standards that make life truly life. This important task, common to all Christians, must be faced with determination. It is the responsibility of Christians, now, to make visible the standards that indicate a just life, which have been clarified for us in Jesus Christ. He has taken up into his life all the words of Scripture: "Listen to him" (Mark 9:7).

And so we come to the third word of our text (1 John 4:9) which I wish to stress: *agape*—love. This is the key word of the whole letter and particularly of the passage which we have heard. *Agape*, love, as St. John teaches us, has nothing of the sentimental or grandiose about it; it is something completely sober and realistic. I attempted to explain something of this in my encyclical *Deus Caritas Est*. Agape love is truly the synthesis of the law and the prophets. In love everything is "fulfilled," but this everything must daily be "filled out." In verse 16 of our text we find the marvelous phrase "We know and believe the love God has for us." Yes, man can believe in love. Let us bear witness to our faith in such a way that it shines forth as the power of love, "so that the world may believe" (John 17:21). Amen!

—Homily, September 12, 2006